ECONOMIC ISSUES, PROBLEMS AND PERSPECTIVES

MUNICIPAL SECURITIES

MARKETS, REGULATION, AND DISCLOSURE

Economic Issues, Problems and Perspectives

Additional books in this series can be found on Nova's website under the Series tab.

Additional e-books in this series can be found on Nova's website under the e-books tab.

Monetary, Fiscal and Trade Policies

Additional books in this series can be found on Nova's website under the Series tab.

Additional e-books in this series can be found on Nova's website under the e-books tab.

ECONOMIC ISSUES, PROBLEMS AND PERSPECTIVES

MUNICIPAL SECURITIES

MARKETS, REGULATION, AND DISCLOSURE

ADAM HARPER
AND
FRANKLIN G. LAWSON
EDITORS

nova publishers
New York

For permission to use material from this book please contact us:
Telephone 631-231-7269; Fax 631-231-8175
Web Site: http://www.novapublishers.com

Additional color graphics may be available in the e-book version of this book.

Library of Congress Cataloging-in-Publication Data

ISBN: 978-1-62257-820-7

Published by Nova Science Publishers, Inc. + New York

CONTENTS

PREFACE

Municipal securities are debt instruments that state and local governments typically issue to finance diverse projects. Individual investors, through direct purchases or investment funds, own 75% of the estimated $3.7 trillion in municipal securities in the U.S. market. In the secondary market, where these securities are bought and sold after issuance, trading largely occurs in over-the-counter markets that are less liquid and less transparent than the exchange-traded equity securities market. The Dodd-Frank Wall Street Reform Act required GAO to review several aspects of the municipal securities market, including the mechanisms for trading, price discovery, and price transparency. This book examines municipal security trading in the secondary market and the factors that affect the prices investors receive and the SEC and self regulatory organizations' enforcement of rules on fair pricing and timely reporting.

Chapter 1 – Municipal securities are debt instruments that state and local governments typically issue to finance diverse projects. Individual investors, through direct purchases or investment funds, own 75 percent of the estimated $3.7 trillion in municipal securities in the U.S. market. In the secondary market, where these securities are bought and sold after issuance, trading largely occurs in over-the-counter markets that are less liquid and less transparent than the exchange-traded equity securities market. The Dodd-Frank Wall Street Reform and Consumer Protection Act required GAO to review several aspects of the municipal securities market, including the mechanisms for trading, price discovery, and price transparency. This report examines (1) municipal security trading in the secondary market and the factors that affect the prices investors receive, and (2) the Securities and Exchange Commission's (SEC) and self- regulatory organizations' (SRO) enforcement of rules on fair pricing and timely reporting.

For this work, GAO analyzed trade data, reviewed federal regulators' programs for enforcing trading rules, and interviewed market participants and federal regulators.

Chapter 2 – Municipal securities are debt instruments that state and local governments issue to finance diverse public projects. As of March 31, 2012, individual investors held up to 75 percent of the total value of municipal securities outstanding. These securities are exempt from certain federal disclosure requirements applicable to other securities sold publicly. Disclosure provided in the primary market, where these securities are issued, generally consists of official statements. Continuing disclosure is information provided in the secondary market, where these securities are bought and sold after issuance. The Dodd-Frank Wall Street Reform and Consumer Protection Act required GAO to review the information issuers of municipal securities must disclose for the benefit of investors. This report addresses (1) the extent to which information currently provided on municipal securities is useful for investors and the extent to which existing regulations reflect principles for effective disclosure, and (2) options for improving the information issuers disclose to investors of municipal securities. To conduct this work, GAO reviewed disclosure rules and compared them with principles for effective disclosure cited by SEC and the International Organization of Securities Commissions, surveyed selected experts and market participants, and interviewed issuers. GAO provided a draft of this report to SEC, MSRB, and the Financial Industry Regulatory Authority (FINRA). SEC and MSRB provided technical comments, which GAO incorporated, as appropriate. FINRA did not provide comments.

In: Municipal Securities
Editors: A. Harper and F. G. Lawson
ISBN: 978-1-62257-820-7

Chapter 1

MUNICIPAL SECURITIES: OVERVIEW OF MARKET STRUCTURE, PRICING, AND REGULATION*

The United States Government Accountability Office

ABBREVIATIONS

ATS	alternative trading system
CEA	Commodity Exchange Act
CFTC	Commodities Futures Trading Commission
CUSIP	Committee on Uniform Security Identification Procedures
DTC	Depository Trust Company
DTTC	Depository Trust and Clearing Corporation
EMMA	Electronic Municipal Markets Access
ERISA	Employee Retirement Income Security Act of 1974
FDIC	Federal Deposit Insurance Corporation
FINRA	Financial Industry Regulatory Authority
MSIL	Municipal Securities Information Library
MSRB	Municipal Securities Rulemaking Board
NASD	National Association of Securities Dealers

* This is an edited, reformatted and augmented version of The United States Government Accountability Office publication, Report to Congressional Requesters GAO-12-265, dated January 2012.

NBBO	National Best Bid and Offer
NBER	National Bureau of Economic Research
NSCC	National Securities Clearing Corporation
OCC	Office of the Comptroller of the Currency
OCIE	Office of Compliance Inspections and Examinations
OTC	over-the-counter
RTRS	Real-Time Transaction Reporting System
RTTM	Real-Time Trade Matching
SEC	Securities and Exchange Commission
SIFMA	Securities Industry and Financial Markets Association
SMMP	Sophisticated Municipal Market Professional
SRO	self-regulatory organization
SSRN	Social Science Research Network
STAR	System for Tracking Activities for Regulatory Policy and Oversight
STARS	Super Tracking and Reporting System
YTM	yield to maturity

WHY GAO DID THIS STUDY

Municipal securities are debt instruments that state and local governments typically issue to finance diverse projects. Individual investors, through direct purchases or investment funds, own 75 percent of the estimated $3.7 trillion in municipal securities in the U.S. market. In the secondary market, where these securities are bought and sold after issuance, trading largely occurs in over-the-counter markets that are less liquid and less transparent than the exchange-traded equity securities market. The Dodd- Frank Wall Street Reform and Consumer Protection Act required GAO to review several aspects of the municipal securities market, including the mechanisms for trading, price discovery, and price transparency. This report examines (1) municipal security trading in the secondary market and the factors that affect the prices investors receive, and (2) the Securities and Exchange Commission's (SEC) and self-regulatory organizations' (SRO) enforcement of rules on fair pricing and timely reporting.

For this work, GAO analyzed trade data, reviewed federal regulators' programs for enforcing trading rules, and interviewed market participants and federal regulators.

What GAO Recommends

GAO recommends that SEC collect and analyze information on SROs' fixed-income regulatory programs on an ongoing basis to better inform its risk-based inspection approach. SEC agreed, but noted it would need additional resources to conduct more frequent oversight of the SROs. Such ongoing monitoring, however, could help SEC better leverage its resources for inspections.

What GAO Found

In the secondary market for municipal securities, both institutional and individual investors trade through brokers, dealers, and banks (broker-dealers). However, GAO analysis of trade data showed that institutional investors generally trade at more favorable prices than individual investors. Broker-dealers said these differences generally reflected the higher average transaction costs associated with trading individual investors' smaller blocks of securities. Market participants added that institutional investors have more resources, including networks of broker-dealers, and the expertise to independently assess prices.

In recent years, the Municipal Securities Rulemaking Board (MSRB)—an SRO that writes rules regulating the broker-dealers that trade municipal securities—has required timely and public posting of trade prices in an effort to make post-trade price information more widely available.

However, unlike the equities market, the relatively illiquid municipal market lacks centrally posted and continuous quotes, and other sources of pretrade price information are not centralized or publicly available to individual investors.

In 2010, SEC began a review of the municipal securities market, in part to examine pretrade price information. MSRB has also begun a study that includes a review of the market structure to determine whether access to additional pretrade price information could improve pricing and liquidity. Both SEC and MSRB plan to complete these studies in 2012.

Several regulators share responsibility for overseeing the municipal securities market.

The Financial Industry Regulatory Authority (FINRA)—an SRO that regulates 98 percent of the broker-dealers that trade municipal securities—and federal banking regulators enforce broker-dealer compliance with MSRB rules under their respective jurisdictions through electronic surveillances of trade data and routine examinations. SEC evaluates the quality of FINRA and MSRB's municipal regulatory programs through its SRO inspection program, which has recently evolved to a risk-based approach. SEC last inspected MSRB and FINRA's fixed-income surveillance program, which encompass municipal securities trading, in 2005. SEC staff said that staffing constraints have prevented them from conducting inspections of these SROs sooner, although they have recently begun a new inspection of FINRA's fixed-income surveillance program. SEC's limited monitoring of FINRA and MSRB between inspections may not be sufficient to support its new risk-based inspection approach.

For example, SEC's last inspection of FINRA's fixed-income surveillance program predated the financial crisis—and its ensuing volatility in the municipal market— but SEC had collected limited information since its last inspection that would help it assess the quality of FINRA's broker-dealer oversight.

SEC currently receives periodic reports from FINRA that provide statistical information on its regulatory activities related to municipal securities trading.

According to SEC staff, while they might be able to use the reports to identify significant deviations in FINRA's efforts, they cannot use them solely to determine the effectiveness of FINRA's municipal securities program. Without ongoing collection and analysis of information to assess the effectiveness of SROs' regulatory programs, SEC may be unable to identify and act on regulatory problems in a timely manner.

January 17, 2012

The Honorable Tim Johnson
Chairman

The Honorable Richard C. Shelby
Ranking Member
Committee on Banking, Housing, and Urban Affairs
United States Senate

The Honorable Spencer Bachus
Chairman

The Honorable Barney Frank
Ranking Member
Committee on Financial Services House of Representatives

Municipal securities are debt instruments that state and local governments issue to finance transportation, housing, hospitals, education, and diverse other projects. The market for these securities is worth an estimated $3.7 trillion, with individuals holding 75 percent of the total outstanding, either indirectly through investment funds or directly through purchases with broker-dealers.[1] But the size, heterogeneity, and other characteristics of this market create challenges, especially in terms of pricing. For example, municipal securities are traded primarily through decentralized, dealer-mediated, over-the-counter (OTC) markets that provide less liquidity and less price transparency than other securities markets, such as the exchange-traded equity market.[2] There is no central facility that publicly posts quotes on all securities trading, as there is in some equities markets. The relative lack of pretrade transparency in the municipal securities market has raised questions about whether individual investors, that is, those who buy and sell securities for themselves directly through broker-dealers, have sufficient price information to make well-informed investment decisions regarding the securities they wish to buy and sell in the secondary market, where municipal securities are traded after they are issued.

The Municipal Securities Rulemaking Board (MSRB) is a self-regulatory organization (SRO) that writes rules regulating the brokers, dealers, and banks (collectively referred to as broker-dealers in this report) that underwrite, sell, and trade municipal securities.[3] MSRB has also issued a number of rules governing municipal trades. Among other things, these rules require broker-dealers to trade municipal securities for their investor customers at fair and reasonable prices and to report their municipal trades in a timely and accurate manner. However, MSRB does not have the authority to enforce these rules and relies instead on the Financial Industry Regulatory Authority, Inc. (FINRA)—an SRO for broker-dealers, federal banking regulators, and the Securities and Exchange Commission (SEC). SEC also provides oversight of MSRB and FINRA.[4]

Title IX of the Dodd-Frank Wall Street Reform and Consumer Protection Act (Dodd-Frank Act) required us to review several aspects of the municipal securities market, including the mechanisms for trading, trade reporting, price discovery, clearance and settlement, and transparency, as well as the potential uses of derivatives in this market.[5] Accordingly, the objectives of this report are to (1) analyze how investors trade municipal securities in the secondary market and the factors affecting the prices they receive, and (2) determine how federal regulators enforce MSRB rules to help ensure fair and reasonable prices for investors and the timely and accurate reporting of municipal trades, including recent trends in the enforcement of these rules. We address the potential uses of derivatives by municipal issuers in appendix I of the report.

To address municipal security trading in the secondary market, we analyzed MSRB trade data from the Real-Time Transaction Reporting System (RTRS)—the system to which broker-dealers report their municipal securities trades—for the period from 2005 to 2010. In so doing, we reviewed information from MSRB on the policies and procedures it used to ensure that the data were complete and accurate and determined that the data were reliable for our purpose. In addition, we reviewed studies and industry literature. We interviewed members of trade organizations representing institutional investors (mutual funds and other investment management companies, insurance companies, and banks that possess or control considerable assets for large-scale investing), broker-dealers (including broker's brokers), and individual investors; officials from independent municipal market research and advisory firms; and officials from SEC's Office of Municipal Securities and MSRB.[6] We attended and viewed SEC's field hearings on the state of the municipal securities market. We also received demonstrations of and interviewed officials from an alternative trading system (ATS) specializing in the electronic trading of municipal securities and of Bloomberg, L.P. (Bloomberg), which provides information and other services related to municipal securities trading.

To address the regulators' enforcement of rules on fair pricing and timely reporting, we reviewed MSRB rules and draft rules related to the pricing of municipal securities, trade reporting, and clearance and settlement of municipal securities transactions. We reviewed MSRB data from RTRS on the number of trades that MSRB determined were reported late for each year from January 2005 to July 2011. We reviewed documentation related to FINRA's programs for surveilling RTRS data for potential violations of MSRB pricing and trade reporting rules and examination procedures used by FINRA, federal banking regulators, and SEC's Office of Compliance Inspections and Examinations (OCIE) to assess broker-dealers' compliance with these rules. We reviewed samples of municipal broker-dealer examinations conducted from 2002 to 2010 by OCIE and from 2006 to 2010 by FINRA and federal banking regulators. In addition, we reviewed OCIE's guidance for conducting SRO inspections and reviewed the most recent inspections of MSRB and

FINRA's fixed-income program conducted in 2002 and 2005.[7] We also reviewed OCIE's 2009 inspections of two SROs that clear and settle municipal, corporate, and equity securities transactions—the Depository Trust Company (DTC) and the National Securities Clearing Corporation (NSCC). Further, we looked at relevant documentation pertaining to coordination among the SEC, FINRA, MSRB, and federal banking regulators—the Board of Governors of the Federal Reserve System (Federal Reserve), the Federal Deposit Insurance Corporation (FDIC), and the Office of the Comptroller of the Currency (OCC)—in conducting oversight of the municipal securities market and interviewed officials from these entities.

We conducted this performance audit from November 2010 to January 2012 in accordance with generally accepted government auditing standards. Those standards require that we plan and perform the audit to obtain sufficient, appropriate evidence to provide a reasonable basis for our findings and conclusions based on our audit objectives. Appendix II provides a more detailed description of our scope and methodology.

BACKGROUND

The municipal securities market comprises both primary and secondary markets. In the primary market, underwriters buy new securities from municipal issuers (e.g., local government entities) and subsequently sell them to investors during the primary offering.[8] Municipal securities that trade after the primary offering are said to trade in the secondary market, with both institutions and individuals participating.[9] Institutional investors typically trade municipal securities in amounts of $1 million or more and generally are in the market full-time to provide or preserve income as well as maximize investment returns for their clients or firms. In contrast, individual investors typically trade municipal securities in amounts of $100,000 or less and access the market relatively infrequently, with the intent to buy and hold securities until maturity.[10] Many individual investors find municipal securities an attractive investment option because of the tax advantages these intruments offer. Unlike the dividends on equity securities (which also trade in a market with considerable individual investor participation), the interest on most municipal securities is exempt from federal income tax and, in some cases, from state or local income tax.[11] In addition, as debt instruments municipal securities are generally considered less risky than equity securities. For example, issuers of debt securities have a contractual obligation to return the principal value of the security to the holder at maturity, while issuers of equity securities do not. Further, issuers of debt securities also have a contractual obligation to pay investors a fixed or variable rate of interest income. On the other hand, dividend payments to shareholders of equity securities are decided by the company's board of directors.

Municipal Securities and Secondary Market Structure

Data on the number of municipal issuers and outstanding municipal securities are not officially tracked by regulators or the private sector. Third-party information vendors provide a range of estimates; data we obtained from one indicated the municipal securities market has over 46,000 municipal issuers, including states, counties, cities, towns, and state and local government agencies, among others, and at least 1.1 million securities outstanding.[12] In contrast, about 5,700 public companies list their equity securities for trading on the major U.S. exchanges.[13] Each municipal issuance is unique, with its own credit structure, terms, and conditions.[14] Most outstanding municipal securities trade infrequently—for example, in 2010 about 99 percent of outstanding municipal securities did not trade on any given day.[15] The heaviest trading of municipal securities typically occurs immediately following their issuance, after which trading becomes sporadic.

The municipal securities market is geographically fragmented, with secondary market trading supported by national and regional broker-dealer firms that serve institutional investors (institutional broker-dealers) or individual investors (retail broker-dealers), and in some firms, both. Several national broker-dealer firms have enough capital and geographic presence to underwrite large new issuances nationwide, trade in large volume with institutional investors, and offer expertise in virtually every sector of the market.[16] Some midsized broker-dealer firms also have nationwide coverage for institutional and individual investors on a smaller scale. But other broker-dealer firms provide inventory and expertise in well-defined geographic areas, allowing them to serve individual investors—many of whom invest in municipal securities to enjoy state or local income tax benefits—as well as institutional investors who need access to local markets. Given the heterogeneity and variety of municipal securities available, the fact that they are traded infrequently, and the geographic fragmentation of the market, broker-dealers typically work with their customers to find available securities that fit preferred parameters (e.g., geographic location, yield, credit quality, or price) instead of specific securities. The fact that the average municipal security is traded infrequently indicates that generally ready buyers and sellers are not available. Thus, some broker-dealers provide liquidity for their investors by committing capital to maintain their own inventories. In doing so, these broker-dealers can offer investors securities when they want to buy and buy securities when investors want to sell. Broker-dealers may also facilitate trades taking little or no risk on their own capital by purchasing or selling securities in order to fulfill prearranged orders.[17] In addition to trading securities from their own inventories, broker-dealers communicate and trade securities with other broker-dealers directly to expand the pool of securities that they may offer investors and to find potential buyers for their securities. Such communication can also help them identify market supply and demand trends on particular securities. Broker-dealers generally communicate with each other directly by phone or through Bloomberg, which connects its users through e-mail, instant text, and other features that allow users to share information on and post offerings, obtain and provide bids on securities, and conduct research and analysis. Broker-dealers may also use broker's brokers and electronic trading platforms to trade in the secondary market. Currently, about 20 broker's brokers promote additional liquidity and facilitate information flow in the municipal securities markets by specializing in segments of the market (by region, issuer, or type of security) and helping broker-dealers find buyers for their securities in their areas of expertise.[18] They do so primarily by arranging auctions called bid wanted procedures (bids wanted) for broker-dealers that are selling securities, particularly in unfamiliar areas of the market.[19] Broker-dealers can also buy and sell municipal securities for their customers through electronic trading platforms that combine inventories from market participants, typically broker-dealers, into one location, thus enabling users—mostly broker-dealers and, in some cases, institutional investors—to search for, buy, and sell municipal securities from a single site. Some of these trading platforms focus on trading for the individual investor market. However, individual investors typically do not have direct access to these trading platforms, although they may have indirect access through a retail broker-dealer.[20]

Municipal Market Regulation

About 1,800 securities firms and banks are registered with MSRB as broker-dealers of municipal securities. As an SRO, MSRB develops rules for broker-dealers engaged in underwriting, trading, and selling municipal securities with the goals of protecting investors and issuers and promoting a fair and efficient marketplace.[21] To further its mandate to protect investors, MSRB also operates information systems designed to promote post-trade price transparency and access to municipal securities issuers' disclosure documents. MSRB provides this access free of charge through its Electronic Municipal Markets Access (EMMA) website. As we have seen, FINRA and federal banking regulators enforce MSRB rules for broker-dealers under their respective jurisdictions. FINRA oversees 98 percent of those MSRB-registered broker-dealers that are also registered members of FINRA, while federal baking regulators oversee the remaining 2 percent.

SEC has designated FINRA as the entity responsible for conducting surveillance of trade data from RTRS for potential violations of MSRB rules. FINRA employs automated surveillance in its compliance monitoring that is programmed to review RTRS data for potentially excessive prices and late trading, among other rule violations. FINRA staff review alerts generated by automated surveillance systems to identify those that warrant further investigation. When FINRA finds evidence of potential violations of these rules involving those broker-dealers who are its members, it can take action ranging from informal warnings to the imposition of monetary fines to expulsion from its membership, among other sanctions. FINRA refers potential violations involving bank dealers to the appropriate federal banking regulator. During the period of our review, FINRA and the federal banking regulators conducted routine examinations of the firms under their jurisdiction once every 2 years for compliance with MSRB rules, pursuant to MSRB requirements.[22]

OCIE administers SEC's nationwide examination and inspection program. OCIE oversees the SROs' compliance with federal securities laws and the SROs' enforcement of their members' compliance with federal securities laws and SRO rules through inspections. Inspection review areas include an SRO's compliance, examination, and enforcement programs. OCIE also directly assesses broker-dealer compliance with federal securities laws through examinations such as cause and risk-based examinations. If examiners identify compliance findings during broker-dealer examinations, they may assess the quality of any recent FINRA examinations of the broker-dealer and provide oversight comments to FINRA.

SEC's Office of Municipal Securities is a separate office within the Division of Trading and Markets that coordinates SEC's municipal securities activities, advises on policy matters relating to the municipal security market, and provides technical assistance in the development and implementation of major SEC initiatives in the municipal securities area. In addition, the Office of Municipal Securities reviews and processes rule proposals filed by MSRB and acts as SEC's liaison with MSRB, FINRA, and a variety of industry groups on municipal securities issues. SEC's Division of Enforcement (Enforcement) investigates possible violations of securities laws, recommends commission action when appropriate, either in a federal court or before an administrative law judge, and negotiates settlements. In January 2010, Enforcement created the Municipal Securities and Public Pensions Unit, which focuses on misconduct in the municipal securities market and in connection with public pension funds.

Municipal Securities Are Priced in an Opaque Market That Favors Better-Informed Participants

Because of the heterogeneity of the issuers and the securities they issue, the large number of securities outstanding, and the infrequency with which these securities trade, the municipal securities market does not maintain reliable tradable quotes on all outstanding municipal securities.[23] Consequently, broker-dealers we spoke with said they use a variety of information to determine the prices at which they are willing to buy and sell securities. We found that institutional investors traded at more favorable prices than individual investors and were generally better equipped to make independent assessments of the value of a security. SEC, MSRB, and market participants have been considering ways to improve pretrade price transparency.

Among Other Factors, Broker-Dealers Use Information on Similar Securities to Assess the Relative Value of a Security and Determine Its Price

As we have seen, the large municipal securities market, with its many issuers and infrequent trades for a given security, does not have readily available, transparent information on the prices of securities. Municipal broker-dealers generally determine the prices at which they are willing to trade by making relative assessments of a security's market value, drawing on various sources of information and incorporating their compensation for facilitating the trades.[24] Several factors that broker-dealers we spoke with identified as relevant to their pricing determinations included (1) recent post-trade price information on same or comparable securities, (2) available pretrade price information on the security or comparable securities, (3) the characteristics and credit quality of the security, (4) relevant market information, and (5) the cost of trading the security.

First, when determining prices, broker-dealers said they often began by reviewing recent post-trade information on the same or similar securities. In 2005 MSRB began requiring broker-dealers to report price data on most municipal securities transactions within 15 minutes to RTRS and, in 2008, made this post-trade pricing information freely available on the EMMA website.[25] Broker-dealers we spoke with said that the price of a recently reported interdealer trade for a security was a particularly good indication of its value for that segment of the market.[26] However, if a security has not traded recently, they said they instead look for recent trades in comparable securities. Broker-dealers we spoke with also said they typically access MSRB's trade data through Bloomberg, which makes available tools to perform advanced searches and analytics on the data.

These broker-dealers also said that they frequently used industry benchmarks—typically yield curves—constructed in part from the post-trade prices of selected securities as a reference for pricing similar securities. [27] Representatives of broker-dealers we interviewed explained that post-trade information provided them with an understanding of real-time trends in the demand for similar types of securities. For example, a major electronic trading platform offers several tools for assessing the prices of its listed offerings using post-trade information. Users can see recently reported trades for similar securities, compare the offer price with a widely used benchmark curve, and receive alerts if the offering price exceeds the most recently reported trade by a specified threshold.

Second, broker-dealers may use available pretrade price information on the same or similar securities to infer market value. In the absence of tradable quotes for outstanding securities, pretrade price information in the municipal securities market includes bids from bids wanted and offer prices. However, unlike post-trade information, pretrade price information is not centralized, not publicly available, and not as available to broker-dealers (and to other market participants) as post-trade price information. To estimate the market value for a security they want to sell, broker-dealers may solicit bids—or may ask a broker's broker to solicit bids— through a bid wanted. Broker's brokers may also provide broker-dealers with otherwise publicly unavailable information on third-party bids and offers from past bids wanted as well as the highest bid and the lowest offer available at a given time for securities in their areas of expertise. For example, a broker's broker who regularly puts a security out for bid wanted can provide information to broker-dealers on the bids received even if the security has not traded in the last 2 months. Additionally, broker-dealers obtain information about offer prices mainly through their relationships and daily communications with other broker-dealers or broker's brokers, their investors who may inform them of competing offers, and listed offerings on electronic trading platforms or Bloomberg.

Third, information on the credit quality of a security may affect its market value, particularly any changes to the credit quality of the security since it last traded. Broker-dealers can infer the credit quality of a security by reviewing information from issuers' financial disclosures posted on the EMMA website, which they typically access via Bloomberg. Issuer disclosures that may affect a security's market value include information on principal and interest payment delinquencies, changes in credit ratings, and unscheduled draws on debt service reserves reflecting financial difficulties, among other factors. Broker-dealers stated that their ability to understand the credit risk of a particular security rested primarily on their ability to obtain timely, comprehensive issuer disclosures. However, they noted that municipal issuers' disclosures are sometimes outdated and incomplete.[28] They added that conducting an independent assessment of the credit quality of municipal securities has become increasingly important given the decline in the availability and use of bond insurance following the recent financial crisis.[29]

Fourth, broker-dealers identified overall market conditions and events as important factors to consider when inferring the market value of a security. For example, an increase in interest rates since the last time a security has traded will, other things being equal, reduce its value.[30] Another important factor broker-dealers consider is overall supply and demand. For example, broker-dealers we interviewed told us that they monitored the primary market because investor demand for new issues affects prices for similar securities in the secondary market. Broker-dealers also told us that by being visible and frequently transacting in the market, they could maintain continuous dialogue with their customers about prices, helping to gauge the interest of investors and other broker-dealers in certain securities at given prices. Finally, broker-dealers said that external factors such as "headline risk"—the risk that a news story will affect prices in a market—can also affect prices in the municipal securities market. An example of headline risk cited by broker-dealers we interviewed was a December 2010 report by a financial markets analyst predicting widespread defaults among municipal issuers. This report caused many individual investors to withdraw their money from these funds, in turn depressing prices.

Fifth, in determining prices, broker-dealers we spoke with said they typically consider trading costs associated with every municipal securities trade, such as fees to MSRB, and operational costs. They said that in general, it is less costly for broker-dealers to trade a given volume of securities in a few large blocks than in a large number of small blocks. For example, an institutional broker-dealer with a $2 million block of securities to sell may have to find only one buyer for the securities, while a retail broker-dealer with a similar block of securities might have to find 100 individual investors to purchase these securities in smaller blocks of $20,000. They explained that the higher costs related to the smaller trades include not only the time and other related costs of finding many more interested buyers, but also the risk that the broker-dealer incurs in holding the securities in his inventory during that time. Last, broker-dealers we spoke with told us that they could spend considerable amounts of time with individual investors explaining the characteristics and relative risks of the securities, answering questions, and complying with regulatory requirements that govern broker-dealer transactions with individual investors. In contrast, they said they do not have to spend as much time with institutional investors, who are typically more knowledgeable and experienced market participants. In order to be profitable, broker-dealers consider these costs when establishing prices.

These broker-dealers also noted that they used their professional judgment to determine the weight of any factor in determining the price for a security, given the facts and circumstances surrounding the transaction. For example, while a recent trade price on a similar security may drive a security's trade price in one case, the same information may become less relevant in the case of a security that has more recently suffered a credit downgrade.

Individual Investors Generally Trade at Less Favorable Prices than Institutional Investors

We analyzed MSRB data for secondary market trades involving newly issued fixed-rate securities during the period from 2005 through 2010.[31] We found that (1) relative to institutional investors, individual investors generally paid higher prices when buying—and received lower prices when selling—municipal securities; (2) broker-dealers received larger spreads (i.e., the difference between the purchase and selling price of a security based as a percentage of the purchase price) when trading smaller blocks of municipal securities; and (3) the prices that individual investors paid for a given security tended to be more dispersed—that is, to vary more—than the prices that institutional investors paid.[32]

First, our analysis revealed that for broker-dealer sales to investors, the relative price declined on average with trade amount, and that the opposite occurs for broker-dealer purchases from investors.[33] That is, investors paid higher prices when buying smaller blocks of securities from broker-dealers—and received lower prices when selling them— than they paid or received for larger trades.

Table 1 shows average relative price for trades involving newly issued fixed-rate securities issued in 2010. The table shows that as trade size increased, relative prices that investors paid for municipal securities declined steadily and relative prices that investors received for selling their securities increased steadily. For example, on average, investors paid 101.9 percent of a security's reoffering price and received 99.4 percent of a security's reoffering price for $5,000 worth of securities, while they paid 100.1 percent of a security's reoffering price and received 100.5 percent of a security's reoffering price for $2 million worth of securities.

As discussed earlier, individual investors typically trade municipal securities in amounts of $100,000 or less, and institutional investors typically trade in amounts of $1 million or more. Consequently, individual investors are likely paying higher prices than institutional investors when they purchase municipal securities and receiving lower prices than institutional investors when they sell municipal securities.

Our analysis also found that broker-dealers received larger spreads when trading small blocks of municipal securities.[34] Because individual investors tend to trade smaller amounts than institutional investors, individual investors tended to pay higher spreads than institutional investors. For example, our analysis showed that the average spread for a $20,000 trade of a fixed-rate security in 2010 was around 2 percent and for a $5 million trade around 0.01 percent.

Table 2 shows how these spreads affect investors' return as measured by the yield to maturity (the yield received after the security matures) on two hypothetical trades of $20,000 and $5 million of the same securities purchased by an individual investor and an institutional investor, respectively.

Table 1. Average Relative Prices on Newly Issued Fixed-Rate Municipal Securities, by Trade Amount, 2010

Trade amount	Average relative prices for broker-dealer sales to Investors (%)[a]	Average relative prices for broker-dealer purchases from investors (%)
$1,000-$10,000	101.9	99.4
$10,000-$20,000	101.8	99.6
$20,000-$50,000	101.4	99.7
$50,000-$100,000	100.9	100.1
$100,000-$250,000	100.4	100.1
$250,000-$500,000	100.3	100.3
$500,000-$1 million	100.2	100.4
$1 million-$5 million	100.1	100.5
$5 million and over	100.1	100.5

Source: GAO analysis of MSRB trade data.

[a]The relative price on a municipal security is the trade price expressed as a percentage of the reoffering price. We analyzed trades that occurred within the period from 30 days prior to 120 days after the dated date (date from which interests start to accrue) on municipal securities that had dated dates in 2010. We analyzed trades involving fixed-rate securities and excluded trades involving zero-coupon or variable-rate securities. The largest trade in 2010 in the sample was for $6.1 million.

Table 2. Example of Broker-Dealer Spreads' Effects on the Yields to Maturity Received by an Individual and an Institutional Investor

	Broker-dealer retail-sized purchase	Broker-dealer sale to individual investor with 2% spread	Broker-dealer institutional-sized purchase	Broker-dealer sale to institutional investor with 0.01% spread
Par value	$20,000	$20,000	$5,000,000	$5,000,000
Coupon rate	5.00%	5.00%	5.00%	5.00%
Years to maturity	10	10	10	10
Par value price	$100.00	$102.00	$100.00	$100.01
Total price	$20,000	$20,400	$5,000,000	$5,000,500
Yield to maturity (YTM)	5.00%	4.75%	5.000%	4.99%
Percentage change in YTM		-5.07%		-0.03%

Source: GAO.

In addition, our analysis showed a wider range of prices for smaller trades than for larger trades from 2005 through 2010. That is, prices for larger trades tended to be more concentrated, while prices for smaller trades tended to be more dispersed. To the extent that individual investors trade smaller amounts than institutional investors, this relationship indicates that individual investors were more likely to pay a wider spectrum of prices for a given security than institutional investors. Table 3 shows price dispersion for trades involving newly issued fixed-rate municipal securities issued in 2010. The table shows prices that investors paid (and, to a lesser extent, received) for municipal securities were more dispersed for smaller trades than for larger trades.

Table 3. Average Price Dispersion for Newly Issued Fixed-Rate Municipal Securities, 2010

Trade amount	Average price dispersion for broker-dealer sales to investors (%)[a]	Average price dispersion for broker-dealer purchases from investors (%)
$1,000-$10,000	1.24	0.68
$10,000-$20,000	1.05	0.43
$20,000-$50,000	0.88	0.46
$50,000-$100,000	0.46	0.33
$100,000-$250,000	0.18	0.19
$250,000-$500,000	0.13	0.19
$500,000-$1 million	0.11	0.25
$1 million-$5 million	0.11	0.27
$5 million and over	0.07	0.07

Source: GAO analysis of MSRB trade data.

[a]Price dispersion is the difference between the maximum and minimum trade price for a security as a percentage of its average trade price. We analyzed trades that occurred within the period from 30 days prior to 120 days after the dated date on municipal securities with dated dates in 2010. We analyzed trades involving fixed-rate securities and excluded trades involving zero coupon or variable-rate securities. The largest trade in 2010 in the sample was for $6.1 million. Our results were statistically significantly at the 1 percent level for all years.

These findings are consistent with previous research on municipal securities trades. For example, researchers analyzing trades of municipal securities found that broker-dealers received larger spreads on smaller trades than they received on larger trades.[35] In addition, researchers analyzing trades of recently issued municipal securities found that prices for smaller trades were more dispersed than prices for larger trades.[36]

Individual Investors Generally Have Less Information and Expertise to Assess Prices than Institutional Investors

Various factors could contribute to the differences in prices that individual investors receive relative to institutional investors. Some researchers have suggested that these differences are not entirely accounted for by differences in dealer costs between large and small trades. One study suggests the lower spreads that institutional investors pay may also be due to the lack of price transparency in the market, which allows better informed investors to obtain more favorable trade prices.[37] Another study adds that institutional investors' continuous engagement in the market and frequent interaction with broker-dealers also provide them with more bargaining power than individual investors. This study also suggests that the more dispersed prices that individual investors experience could indicate that, in the nontransparent municipal securities market, broker-dealers may have more opportunities to charge higher prices when dealing with less knowledgeable investors. The authors explained that the wider range of prices individual investors receive when they buy or sell the same security could reflect broker-dealers' ability to detect diverse levels of sophistication among individual investors, with less knowledgeable individuals potentially more likely to trade at less favorable prices than more market-savvy individuals.[38]

A third study, however, concludes that differences in prices are not entirely due to the lack of transparency in this market. The study notes that municipal securities often pass through a chain of dealers before being placed with investors and suggests that such interdealer trading may contribute to differences in prices for individual and institutional investors. This study finds that the prices investors pay increase with the amount of interdealer trading that preceded their purchases, and also that more interdealer trading is associated with greater price dispersion. The study also finds that successive interdealer trades tend to involve smaller and smaller trades, thus suggesting that investors trading smaller amounts—individual investors—are likely to pay higher prices and also more dispersed prices than investors trading larger amounts—institutional investors.[39]

We found several factors that likely affected individual investors' ability to gain and use information to independently assess offers and bids they received from their broker-dealers for municipal securities they were interested in purchasing or selling. While MSRB has increased the amount of information available to all investors through its EMMA website—including price information on past trades and issuer disclosures—institutional investors we spoke with generally had more resources and expertise to assess prices than individual investors. In particular, they had (1) access to more sources of pretrade price information in the form of offerings and bids provided through their large networks of broker-dealers, (2) access to more user-friendly post-trade information through third-party vendors and their networks of broker-dealers, and (3) more market expertise to help them incorporate other available information.

Institutional Investors Generally Have Access to More Sources of Pretrade Price Information

First, institutional investors told us that when buying securities they accessed the fragmented municipal market through their large networks of broker-dealers. For the institutional investors we interviewed, these networks range from 30 to over 100 national and regional broker-dealers who compete for their business by providing them with a wide range of municipal securities offerings from the primary and secondary markets.[40] For example, institutional investors typically receive daily secondary market offerings from their broker-dealers through Bloomberg, which provides an interface that allows users to pull together and organize these offerings for easy analysis—an important feature in a large, heterogeneous market where price discovery depends heavily on relative assessments of similar securities.

Relative to institutional investors, individual investors typically have access to fewer sources of pretrade price information. Unlike institutional investors that have access to and can compare thousands of daily offerings from their large networks of broker-dealers, individuals typically have brokerage accounts with a few broker-dealers, perhaps only one, that may or may not offer online access to their offerings.[41] Individuals with online access to a brokerage firm's offerings can search for securities that meet certain parameters and compare the results. They may be able to repeat this exercise with other broker-dealers, although they are unlikely to obtain competing prices for the same security.[42] In contrast, some investors without access to online offerings told us that they relied on their broker-dealers. These investors can compare prices of similar securities only insofar as their brokers share this information with them. However, some retail broker-dealer firms have taken steps to attract individual investors by combining offerings from electronic trading platforms with their own offerings, thus expanding the pool of securities available to their customers.[43] According to one of the largest municipal electronic trading platforms, which caters to retail broker-dealers, individuals can access the platform's inventory through several major brokers, most full-service brokers, and many independent financial advisers.[44]

Similarly, institutional investors wanting to sell municipal securities generally have multiple ways to obtain pretrade price information in the form of bids. Their access to large networks of broker-dealers and tools for obtaining bids from more than one dealer allows them to contact potential buyers and independently assess the bids they receive for their securities. Institutional investors we interviewed said that they also frequently carried out their own bids wanted by using Bloomberg to solicit bids from broker-dealers in order to gauge demand and potentially receive a bid at which they were willing to sell.[45] Additionally, these institutional investors told us that they might offer securities directly to broker-dealers to find interested parties among the firms or their customers. Finally, institutional investors can ask a broker-dealer to offer the security for sale through a broker's broker or an electronic trading platform.[46]

By contrast, individual investors typically do not have independent access to multiple bids and thus may be less able to assess the prices they receive for securities they want to sell. When individuals sell securities, they typically rely on the broker-dealer responsible for the account that houses the securities to find a market. A retail broker-dealer may offer the securities to other broker-dealers or customers or may solicit bids through a broker's broker or an electronic trading platform. However, because selling small blocks of securities is generally more difficult than selling larger blocks, broker-dealers we interviewed said that they might be able to obtain only a few bids for the individual investor. Although the broker-dealer may explain to the individual his process for obtaining bids, individual investors may have difficulty judging the level of demand for their securities or the level of effort their broker-dealers made to find potential buyers.

Institutional Investors Can Access Post-trade Pricing Information through the EMMA Website, Bloomberg, and Their Broker-Dealers

Similar to broker-dealers, institutional investors we interviewed told us that they can access MSRB's historical trade information through the EMMA website and centrally through Bloomberg, which allows users to compare post-trade prices for two or more securities that share similar characteristics using a search function. Institutional investors also said that their established relationships and continued negotiation with their broker-dealers often revealed market patterns from post-trade prices that helped them assess prices. For example, some large institutional investors told us that broker-dealers typically let them know about large or otherwise meaningful trades that they believed might affect prices of similar securities before these trades appeared on RTRS (postings must occur within 15 minutes of the trade). Some of these investors said that even though MSRB's RTRS system did not disclose total transaction amounts for trades over $1 million—which the system reports as trade amounts of "$1+ million"—they typically were aware of the amount and the price of these large transactions through their relationships with broker-dealers. Market participants have said that this information is important, because prices in large trades affect prices for many other similar securities because of the relative nature of pricing in this market. Institutional investors are also able to benefit from broker-dealers' commentaries on trades or on demand trends in the market through Bloomberg.

In contrast, individuals—who are likely to find Bloomberg prohibitively expensive—can obtain post-trade information on any outstanding security from the EMMA website but may encounter limitations.[47] While individual investors may use the EMMA website to look for past trade prices of a security to assess the current price, this information is likely not useful unless the latest trade is relatively recent, as we have seen. Currently, the EMMA website does not have search capabilities designed to allow users to identify comparable securities. Further, individual investors could misinterpret post-trade pricing data if they were unaware that reported prices for investor transactions reflected dealers' compensation for the trade as well as the estimated market value of the security. MSRB is currently evaluating improvements that would make the EMMA website more meaningful and useful for individual investors.[48]

Institutional Investors' Market Expertise Allows Them to Better Use Available Information to Assess Prices

Institutional investors we spoke with generally employed professional staff, such as credit analysts and traders, who specialized in evaluating credit risk and trading municipal securities and maintained models to evaluate offering prices.[49] Institutional investors we interviewed stated that in general they could form an immediate initial judgment about the price of a municipal security because they were entrenched in the market on a daily basis and had accumulated expertise to inform their decision making. These investors told us that they applied a wealth of market history to determine a security's relative value. They said that, for example, they knew the approximate price at which an A-rated hospital security in California with a 30-year maturity is trading and could update prices for the same or similar securities by looking at technical features (like call features), the issuers' financial profile, and the market strength on the day of the trade, among other things.

By contrast, individual investors have access to issuer financial disclosures through MSRB's EMMA website and other publicly available issuer information but may lack the expertise to understand and update prices using this information. Besides issuer disclosures, individuals have access to free investor information websites, such as the Securities Industry and Financial Markets Association's (SIFMA) investinginbonds.com, which makes available various market benchmark yield curves, among other things. Many of these resources may also be available to individuals through their broker-dealers' online websites. However, some institutional investors we spoke with believed that professional expertise was required to use this information to assess prices, especially for securities that had not traded recently. For example, even with timely access to issuer disclosures, it is not clear that individual investors with relatively limited market expertise would be able to estimate how a rating downgrade translated into a lower price for a security.[50]

Additionally, individual investors may undertake varied degrees of research during the few hours that they typically have to make an investment decision. For example, some investors we spoke with did not look at historical trade information or issuer disclosure information when they bought bonds and instead relied on the recommendation of their broker-dealer. Others, however, chose a few potential securities from their broker-dealer's online offerings and checked historical trade information and disclosure information for those securities. One of the more knowledgeable among the individual investors we spoke with stated that he treated the last interdealer trade price as a benchmark for pricing and used this information with varying degrees of success to negotiate prices with brokers. For example, one individual said he had successfully used the last traded price to bargain for better prices with his broker and found that if he was buying bonds for a par value of $200,000, for example, he might be able to save $100 (or 0.05 percent of par value).

Market participants explained that individual investors faced additional challenges in independently assessing the value of a security since the decline in the use and availability of bond insurance following the recent financial crisis. In the past, individual investors could choose to buy an insured security and rely on the insurer's guarantee without fully understanding the security's underlying value. Individual investors may review issuer disclosures through the EMMA website to help in independently assessing risk, but some individual investors have expressed frustration at their inability to identify and understand the relevant pieces of information from the typically long and technical issuer disclosures.[51]

SEC, MSRB, and Market Participants Are Considering Ways to Improve Pretrade Price Transparency

SEC and MSRB have ongoing studies examining the municipal security market. In May 2010, SEC announced that it was beginning a review of the municipal securities markets and intended to examine pretrade price transparency, among other issues, using a series of field hearings.[52] At the conclusion of the review, SEC staff are to prepare a publicly available report recommending whether specific changes to laws, regulation, or private sector best practices are needed to better protect municipal securities investors. SEC staff anticipate that the report will be finalized and made public in 2012. In December 2010, MSRB also announced that it was undertaking a study of the municipal securities market, including a review of market structure and trading patterns. MSRB stated that the study would include a review of transaction costs, price dispersion, and other market data and was intended to help MSRB assess whether the market was operating as efficiently and fairly as possible. It is also intended to assist MSRB in evaluating whether pricing and liquidity in the market could be improved with higher levels of pretrade price transparency. MSRB staff said that the initial phase of the study would likely be completed in 2012. MSRB said that in considering whether to recommend potential changes in terms of market structure or disclosures that would improve price transparency, the costs and benefits would need to be weighed carefully.

Discussions to improve pretrade price transparency in the municipal securities market focus on whether and how to make bid and offer information on municipal securities more widely available and how to improve individual investors' access to the market. In an October 2010 speech discussing SEC's review of the municipal securities markets, one commissioner noted that post-trade transparency in this market had improved considerably since MSRB's implementation of real-time trade reporting and the EMMA website.[53] However, because of the low liquidity levels of many municipal securities, these trade data could be weeks or months old and therefore not helpful to investors. In part for this reason, the commissioner said, improving pretrade transparency was an important goal. MSRB staff observed that only a few limited venues allowed even knowledgeable and experienced market participants such as broker-dealers to see bid and offer information for municipal trades. They added that because the municipal securities market operates through over-the-counter trading, even the broker-dealers could not see bid and offer information for the entire market.

One challenge to improving pretrade price transparency is determining whether and how to make this information available to the general public in a timely manner, particularly for thinly traded securities. That is, given that most municipal bonds are traded infrequently once they have been initially distributed, two-sided quotes are not continuously available in this market. One suggestion that arose was to create a national listing service where all municipal broker-dealers could list their entire municipal securities offerings for public viewing and allow investors to search for securities that fit their investment parameters and to compare prices and yields. To make selling securities easier for investors, one field hearing participant suggested allowing investors to place bids on offerings, while another suggested establishing a limit order mechanism for this market. [54] These suggestions would necessitate creating a centralized trading venue. However, as of January 2012, market participants had not developed detailed proposals that describe the feasibility or offer cost-benefit analyses of such changes to the structure of the market.

Market participants and observers we spoke to disagreed on the feasibility of creating and maintaining a municipal securities exchange. Some believed that pricing and liquidity in the municipal securities market could be improved through exchange trading, particularly for individual investors.[55] For example, one market participant noted that when buying securities, broker-dealers and investors currently have access to a limited set of offerings in the market, and that when selling securities, they currently only have access to a subset of potential bidders for the securities. This market participant said that an exchange could broaden both broker-dealers' and investors' access to bids and offers for municipal securities, and that such centralized transparent aggregation of dealer and individual investor interest would lead to increased liquidity, even in the absence of two-sided quotes for most bonds. Further, this market participant said that an exchange would promote pretrade price transparency through the public dissemination of bid and offer information. Other market participants agreed that an exchange would broaden individual investors' access to the market and noted that an exchange would allow them to more easily find offerings for comparable securities with the characteristics they wanted. Furthermore, one market expert stated that an exchange would provide more liquidity to investors by taking advantage of existing technology to identify potential interested buyers for a given security, even in the absence of two-sided quotes.

However, broker-dealers and large institutional investors we interviewed stated that, in this fragmented market driven by supply and demand, relationships and direct negotiation were the key to making markets and determining prices. Broker-dealers also pointed to the large number of heterogeneous and relatively illiquid municipal securities that would make it difficult to establish ready two-sided markets for a given security. Additionally, large institutional investors we spoke with stated that a municipal securities exchange may not be feasible or advisable because of the costs of developing a central meeting place that could incorporate these unique attributes of the market. Broker's brokers also thought the negotiated nature of the market limited the feasibility of an exchange and noted that demand for their services had increased greatly with the decline in the availability and use of bond insurance. They said that because broker-dealers could no longer rely on the homogenizing effects of bond insurance, their need for reliable information on, for example, specialized securities' credit and sector trends had increased.

Regulators Oversee Compliance with MSRB Rules and Have Not Found Systemic Violations, but SEC's Monitoring Is Limited

MSRB has issued rules addressing broker-dealers' pricing, trade reporting, and clearance and settlement responsibilities with respect to municipal securities transactions. However, because MSRB does not have enforcement authority over broker-dealers, FINRA, federal banking regulators, and SEC conduct broker-dealer oversight and enforce MSRB rules. FINRA oversees 98 percent of broker-dealers registered with MSRB, and the federal banking regulators (OCC, FDIC, and the Federal Reserve) oversee the remaining 2 percent, which we refer to in this report as bank dealers.[56] SEC's OCIE provides oversight of MSRB and FINRA's regulatory activities. We found that FINRA and the banking regulators did not identify many violations of the pricing and trade reporting rules from 2006 through 2010 and that settlement failures on municipal securities transactions were rare.[57] We also found that, although OCIE conducted multiple FINRA district office inspections and broker-dealer examinations as part of its municipal market oversight, it had not inspected MSRB or FINRA's fixed-income program since 2005 and lacked a program for conducting interim monitoring to assess risks at these SROs.

MSRB Rules Govern Municipal Transaction Pricing, Reporting, and Clearance and Settlement

Several MSRB rules govern broker-dealers with regard to municipal trade pricing, reporting, and clearance and settlement.

- Rule G-30: MSRB Rule G-30 requires that broker-dealers charge fair and reasonable aggregate prices to customers (individual and institutional investors) for buying and selling securities. In principal transactions, in which broker-dealers take securities into their own accounts, the aggregate price reflects not only the market value of the security, but also the compensation the broker-dealer receives on the transaction, either a markup or markdown from the security's prevailing market price.58 A markup is compensation for selling a security to a customer, while a markdown is compensation for buying a security from a customer. A security's prevailing market price is its interdealer market value—or the price at which a broker-dealer would sell or buy the security to or from another broker-dealer—at the time of the customer transaction. Most broker-dealers engage in municipal securities transactions in a principal capacity, and as such are not required to break out the markup or markdown from their aggregate prices. Figure 1 shows how markups and markdowns are calculated and illustrates the markups and markdowns in hypothetical municipal securities transactions. MSRB has stated that, in order to be fair and reasonable, the price of a security must bear a reasonable relationship to its prevailing market price. Both the price and the markup or markdown must be fair and reasonable in order to satisfy Rule G-30. In other words, a broker-dealer cannot charge the prevailing market price but add an excessive markup and still be in compliance with the rule. Citing the heterogeneous nature of municipal securities transactions and broker-dealers, MSRB has not set specific numeric guidelines for acceptable markups or markdowns.59 Since the early 1970s, however, several SEC cases and opinions have addressed instances in which broker-dealers charged excessive aggregate prices. Appendix V describes the key features of several of these cases.

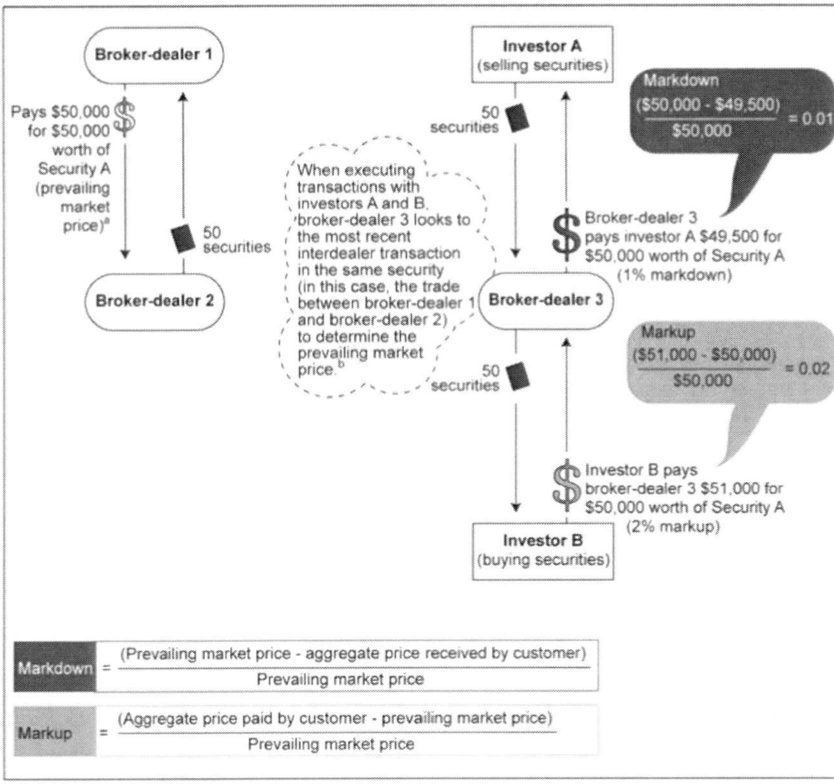

Source: GAO.

[a]The prevailing market price is not necessarily equivalent to par value, as it is in this example.

[b]This example is based on the assumption that no changes occurred in the market between the interdealer transaction and broker-dealer 3's transactions with investors A and B that would affect the prevailing market price.

Figure 1. Hypothetical Broker-Dealer Markups and Markdowns in Municipal Securities Transactions.

- *Rule G-14:* Since 2005, MSRB Rule G-14 has required real-time reporting of most municipal securities trades for transparency and regulatory purposes. With few exceptions, Rule G-14 requires broker-dealers to report all trades to an RTRS portal "promptly, accurately, and completely." [60] In general, reporting to an RTRS portal entails recording transactions and their relevant details within 15 minutes of the time of trade.[61] In addition, Rule G-14 states that broker-dealers must have a current Form RTRS on file with MSRB with the information necessary to ensure that their trade reports can be processed correctly.

- *Rules G-15 and G-12:* MSRB rules provide for most secondary market transactions to settle, or complete delivery and payment, by the third business day following the trade date. Specifically, MSRB Rule G-15 sets out settlement dates with respect to broker-dealers' transactions with customers, while Rule G-12 sets out settlement dates for interdealer municipal transactions.

Regulators Use Various Methods to Monitor and Enforce Compliance with MSRB Pricing and Trade Reporting Rules

MSRB makes trade data submitted by broker-dealers through the RTRS available to FINRA, the federal banking regulators, and SEC for their regulatory activities. In January 2010, MSRB launched Regulator Web, or RegWeb, a secure web-based portal to municipal securities transaction data. RegWeb provides regulators with consolidated access to information including real-time, individual firm transaction data as well as dealer data quality reports (monthly reports listing each dealer's late, canceled, and amended trade statistics); monthly reports on system outages and other statistics; Forms RTRS that firms have filed with MSRB; a list of broker-dealers registered with MSRB; and other information.

FINRA primarily employs an automated surveillance program and conducts examinations of broker-dealers to enforce MSRB rules related to pricing and trade reporting. FINRA uses automated surveillance to monitor all municipal broker-dealers that are FINRA members for compliance with MSRB pricing and trade reporting rules. FINRA's automated surveillance also includes activity related to the bank dealers under the jurisdiction of the federal banking regulators. Using programmed parameters, FINRA assesses RTRS data for potential violations of MSRB rules, including G-30 and G-14. For example, FINRA has surveillance programs that identify transaction prices that appear to be outliers compared with prices in the rest of the market. FINRA analysts follow up on alerts generated by these programs with broker-dealers under its jurisdiction in accordance with written policies and procedures and, in certain circumstances, will refer potential violations by bank dealers to the appropriate federal banking regulator for further investigation. FINRA also assesses compliance with the MSRB pricing and trade reporting rules through routine and cause examinations of municipal broker-dealers. Examiners use an electronic examination module that includes specific instructions for collecting documentation, selecting samples, and running data reports, and for other aspects of their examinations. FINRA's surveillance and examinations can result in a variety of actions against a firm that violates a rule, such as an informal warning or a monetary penalty, among other actions.

The federal banking regulators rely primarily on examinations to monitor bank dealers' compliance with MSRB pricing and trade reporting rules. Officials from these agencies explained that they did not have formal surveillance programs designed to monitor bank dealers' compliance with MSRB rules. Rather, they periodically review MSRB reports on data quality and pricing volatility in RegWeb, often as part of their preparation for on-site examinations. In addition, although the federal banking regulators all stated that such instances are rare, FINRA may refer to them potential violations by bank dealers that it identifies through its automated surveillance program. During their on-site examinations, bank examiners generally take samples of bank dealers' transactions and review them for compliance with Rules G-30 and G-14. Their examinations can result in corrective actions, among other responses.

As part of its oversight of FINRA's regulatory operations, OCIE assesses broker-dealers' compliance with MSRB Rules G-30 and G-14 through broker-dealer examinations. OCIE also may review for compliance with these rules in other types of examinations, such as cause examinations and risk-targeted examinations. Because OCIE uses a risk-based approach to determine areas of focus in these examinations, examiners might not always check for compliance with Rules G-30 and G-14. When they do, however, they follow OCIE's written examination procedures. OCIE's examinations can result in actions such as a deficiency letter to the firm or referral to SEC enforcement staff for a more formal review. See appendix VI for a more detailed description of how FINRA, the federal banking regulators, and OCIE examine for compliance with Rules G-30 and G-14.

MSRB and the other regulators coordinate in various ways to facilitate effective enforcement of Rules G-30 and G-14, as well as other MSRB rules. For example, MSRB officials provided agendas demonstrating that SEC, MSRB, and FINRA have held three semiannual meetings since December 2010, as mandated by the Dodd-Frank Act, to describe their work in the municipal securities market and to discuss any issues related to regulation, including rule interpretation, examinations, and enforcement of MSRB rules. According to documentation provided by MSRB officials, MSRB and FINRA also meet regularly and share information in accordance with a memorandum of understanding, and MSRB meets with SEC several times a year and with the federal banking regulators twice a year to discuss various municipal market issues, with a focus on MSRB rule interpretations, amendments, and guidance.62 In addition to holding formal meetings, SEC, MSRB, and FINRA staff told us that they maintained daily or weekly informal communication to discuss rule filings or interpretations; surveillance, examination, and enforcement issues; technology issues; and other pertinent matters. As described earlier, MSRB also shares RTRS data and other information with the regulators via the RegWeb system. Finally, MSRB officials stated that they provide a variety of training opportunities to examiners and other staff of SEC, FINRA, and other regulators to promote consistency in the enforcement of MSRB rules.

Regulators' Surveillance and Examinations Did Not Reveal Systemic Trade Pricing, Reporting, or Clearance and Settlement Issues

According to our review of regulators' surveillance and examination data, FINRA, the federal banking regulators, and OCIE have identified few violations of Rule G-30 by broker-dealers and bank dealers from 2006 through 2010. Regulatory officials told us that they considered a variety of factors when determining whether a broker-dealer had charged unfair or unreasonable prices, markups, or markdowns. We also found that violations of Rule G-14 were not systemic and that the industry average for late reported trades had decreased substantially since 2005. Finally, sample data from the agency that oversees clearance and settlement of municipal trades indicate that municipal transaction settlement failures are rare.

Trade Pricing

Regulators cited a small number of violations of Rule G-30 during the period from 2006 through 2010. Specifically, FINRA opened 416 reviews based on alerts related to potential G-30 violations occurring during the 5- year review period.[63] FINRA had completed 343 of those reviews by June 2011. Of those 343 reviews:

- FINRA determined that 267 (78 percent) warranted no further review. FINRA officials explained that they had investigated the prices and markups for the firms in question and found that violations had not actually occurred or were too minor to warrant further action.[64]
- Eleven reviews (3 percent) resulted in a cautionary action (an informal warning to the broker-dealer that similar violations in the future could result in formal disciplinary actions).
- One review (less than 1 percent) resulted in a cautionary action for a violation of another MSRB rule.
- Sixty-four (19 percent) were referred internally for potential disciplinary action.

Of the 64 reviews FINRA's surveillance group referred internally, 22 were closed as of June 2011. Of those 22 reviews:

- Two (9 percent) warranted no further review.
- Eight (36 percent) resulted in a cautionary action.
- Twelve (55 percent) resulted in a Letter of Acceptance, Waiver and Consent (a disciplinary action in which the broker-dealer consents to findings and the imposition of sanctions but neither admits nor denies the violations).

Likewise, out of 5,764 examinations with a municipal securities component that FINRA conducted from 2006 through 2010, 51 examinations (less than 1 percent) identified G-30 violations that resulted in a formal or informal action. Of those 51 examinations:

- Thirty-seven (about 73 percent) resulted in a cautionary action.
- Eleven (about 22 percent) resulted in a compliance conference (a more serious type of informal action that involves a meeting between FINRA management and the broker-dealer firm to discuss the violations).
- Three (about 6 percent) were referred internally for potential disciplinary action.[65]

We reviewed 25 of the 51 examinations and found that the markups and markdowns that FINRA questioned in those examinations ranged from about 2 percent to about 10 percent.[66] The federal banking regulators did not report any G-30 violations in the 87 total bank dealer examinations they conducted from 2006 through 2010. OCIE staff also said that, for the examinations they conducted during this time frame in which they assessed broker-dealers for G-30 compliance, they observed a relatively low rate of G-30 violations.[67]

Regulators consider multiple factors in determining broker-dealers' compliance with Rule G-30. For example, Rule G-30 specifies four factors that broker-dealers must consider when determining a fair and reasonable price, including the broker-dealer's best judgment as to the fair market value of the securities at the time of the transaction. In addition, in its interpretive notices, MSRB has identified other factors that may be relevant to this determination, such as the resulting yield—or annual rate of return—of the security to a customer. To determine whether a broker-dealer is in compliance with Rule G-30 on a specific trade, regulators must consider how well the broker-dealer has applied all of the relevant factors as well as the facts and circumstances of the transaction. Table 4 lists the written factors that regulators consider in enforcing this rule. For instance, as part of their consideration of whether broker-dealers use their best judgment in pricing securities, OCIE examiners stated that when they found a potentially excessive markup, they checked to see whether the market had moved or significant information about the issuer had become available just before the transaction.

Table 4. Factors That Regulators Consider in Determining Broker-Dealers' Compliance with MSRB Rule G-30

Source	Factors
Rule G-30	Broker-dealer's best judgment as to the fair market value of the securities at the time of the transaction and of any securities exchanged or traded in connection with the transaction Broker-dealer's expense in effecting the transaction Broker-dealer's entitlement to a profit Total dollar amount of the transaction
MSRB Interpretive Notices	Yield comparable to that on other securities of comparable quality,maturity, coupon rate, and block size then available in the market Maturity of the security Availability of the securities in the market Nature of the broker-dealer's business

Sources: GAO summary of Rule G-30 and MSRB guidance.

We observed how examiners assessed broker-dealers' application of some of these factors in our review of selected FINRA examinations with G-30 violations. For example, FINRA examiners identified six potential G30 violations—all in the form of excessive markups—at one firm they examined. When they asked the firm to explain the markups, which ranged from about 4 percent to nearly 10 percent, the firm stated that all of the transactions in question involved low-rated or unrated bonds and occurred in late 2008, when the market was highly volatile.[68] The firm also stated that because it had no customers for the bonds at the time it purchased them, it had assumed additional risks, and that no comparable interdealer trades were available to establish the prevailing market price. While FINRA examiners concluded that four of the six transactions were fair and reasonable, they cited G-30 violations on the two remaining transactions based on the combination of high markups, firm profits, and the transactions' proximity in time to interdealer purchases. Illustrating the importance of reviewing the individual facts and circumstances in each transaction, examiners deemed one of the highest markups acceptable because the security had been trading within a wide range of prices around the time of the trade in question and the transaction resulted in a high yield to the customer relative to those of comparable securities. In another examination, FINRA examiners questioned a trade in which a firm bought 10 bonds from a customer at a price substantially lower than the last reported trade, which had occurred about a week earlier. The firm indicated that the security's credit rating had dropped within that time period. Given this downgrade and the fact that the bonds in question continued to trade in the lower range for about a month afterward, FINRA examiners determined that the firm had set a fair and reasonable aggregate price and thus had not violated Rule G-30.

In April 2010, MSRB proposed draft guidance that would provide greater specificity for broker-dealers acting as principals in determining a security's prevailing market price. Specifically, MSRB's Regulatory Notice 2010-10 proposed a hierarchical approach that is intended to harmonize with FINRA's approach to pricing nonmunicipal debt securities.[69] The proposed approach would first have the broker-dealer use as the prevailing market price his contemporaneous costs or proceeds—in other words, his costs or proceeds from a transaction recent enough that it would be expected to reflect the current market price for the security. If a broker-dealer wished to use a source other than his contemporaneous costs or proceeds to determine the prevailing market price, he would be required to search through a hierarchy of relevant transactions to seek other appropriate comparison prices. In addition, broker-dealers would be required to document how they determined the prevailing market price in cases where they did not use contemporaneous costs or proceeds. MSRB officials told us that the proposed method would likely make it easier for regulators to conduct surveillance and enforcement for Rule G30, because it would provide a relatively mechanical way to determine a security's prevailing market price. However, broker-dealers have expressed concerns about the proposed method, citing, among other issues, increased burdens and risks to liquidity. As of January 9, 2012, MSRB had not finalized the proposed guidance.[70]

Trade Reporting

Although regulators identified G-14 violations during our review period, these trade reporting issues did not appear to be systemic. According to data we received from MSRB, from February 2005 (the month after the 15-minute reporting requirement took effect) through July 2011, the monthly industry average for late trades declined from approximately 7 percent to less than 1 percent. The average rate of late trades during this time frame was less than 2.5 percent. FINRA officials noted that in 2005 FINRA had assigned a dedicated team to conduct automated surveillance reviews of the municipal market, with an initial focus on late trade reporting. FINRA officials believe that these surveillance efforts likely played a role in the decline of the industry G-14 violation average. FINRA opened 721 reviews based on alerts related to potential G-14 violations occurring from 2006 through 2010. FINRA's surveillance group had completed 621 of those reviews as of June 2011. Of the 621 reviews:

- FINRA determined that 323 (52 percent) required no further review. As with the reviews stemming from G-30 alerts, FINRA officials explained that they had investigated the transaction reports for the firms in question and found that violations had not actually occurred or were too minor to warrant further action.
- Fifty-five (9 percent) resulted in a cautionary action for a G-14 violation.
- Ten (about 2 percent) resulted in a cautionary action for violations of other MSRB rules.
- Another 233 (about 38 percent) were referred internally for potential disciplinary action.

Of the 233 reviews FINRA's surveillance group referred, 147 had been completed as of June 2011:

- Eight (5 percent) warranted no further review.
- Fourteen (about 10 percent) resulted in a cautionary action.
- Three (2 percent) resulted in a minor rule violation plan letter (an informal disciplinary process that allows FINRA to assess fines of less than $2,500).
- The remaining 122 (83 percent) resulted in a Letter of Acceptance, Waiver and Consent.

Also from 2006 through 2010, out of the 5,764 examinations they conducted with a municipal securities component, FINRA examiners cited G-14 violations resulting in a formal or informal action in 910 (about 16 percent). Of those 910 examinations:

- Some 699 (about 77 percent) resulted in a cautionary action.
- Another 136 (15 percent) resulted in a compliance conference.
- Forty-two (about 5 percent) resulted in a Letter of Acceptance, Waiver and Consent.
- The remaining 33 examinations (about 4 percent) resulted in minor rule violation plans, internal referrals for potential disciplinary action, or offers of settlement.

In the sample of 32 FINRA examinations we reviewed with G-14 violations, we found that the violations stemmed from a variety of sources, including human error, deficient procedures, a firm's failure to submit or update a Form RTRS, or technical malfunctions, among other reasons. However, human error and deficient procedures were the most commonly cited causes. Regulators noted that late or inaccurate trade reporting was relatively simple to identify through surveillance and examinations and that broker-dealers could be cited for a G-14 violation based on as little as one or two late or inaccurately reported trades. For example, in one of the FINRA examinations we reviewed, examiners took a sample of 60 trades and found that 2 were reported to MSRB with the incorrect price. A representative of the broker-dealer firm told examiners that the firm had corrected the trades the day they were entered but that an error had led to the suppression of the amended information. FINRA counts instances like this as G-14 violations and requires broker-dealers to update MSRB with the correct information if possible.

The federal banking regulators cited G-14 violations in 8 of the 87 bank dealer examinations they conducted. They generally responded to these violations with corrective action requirements. On the basis of examinations they conducted during this time frame in which they assessed broker-dealers for G-14 compliance, OCIE staff agreed that G14 violations appeared to have decreased in recent years and said that the inadvertent late trades they continued to see were sometimes attributable to factors such as breakdowns in trade reporting systems.

Clearance and Settlement

OCIE staff told us that settlement failures typically appeared to represent a low percentage of municipal transactions cleared through NSCC. According to data gathered during a 5-day trading period in June 2011 by NSCC, municipal trade settlement failures composed approximately 2.1 percent of the total dollar value of all NSCC settlement failures across all markets for that time period.[71]

OCIE Has Not Inspected Key SROs' Municipal Activities since 2005 and Has Conducted Limited Monitoring of SRO Regulatory Efforts

Since 2005, OCIE has not inspected FINRA's fixed-income surveillance program or MSRB, both because of staffing limitations and because of changes to its inspection approach. OCIE's written inspection guidelines call for inspections of MSRB and FINRA's regulatory programs.[72] OCIE did not have a fixed schedule for examining MSRB, but its SRO Inspection Guidelines stated that the office generally inspected each SRO under its jurisdiction every 1-4 years. Until 2010, OCIE conducted routine inspections of various aspects of FINRA's operations—including district office programs, arbitration, customer communication, central review, and financial operations—every 2 to 4 years in accordance with its SRO inspection guidelines. Surveillance, examination, and enforcement programs were typically components of these routine inspections, but municipal securities were not included in each inspection cycle. From 2000 through 2010, mostly in accordance with a 3-year cycle, OCIE conducted 49 inspections of FINRA's district offices, which conduct the majority of broker-dealer examinations. As part of these inspections, they assessed whether FINRA examined municipal securities broker-dealers at least once every 2 years and reviewed a sample of FINRA's workpapers to determine whether FINRA examiners thoroughly reviewed broker-dealers for compliance with all MSRB rules and other applicable rules and regulations.

However, the district office inspections are not intended to address FINRA's surveillance activities or policies and procedures for its municipal market regulatory programs. In 2010, OCIE began transitioning to a risk-based SRO inspection approach in conjunction with a comprehensive assessment of OCIE's structure and functions.[73] As such, OCIE will no longer conduct inspections according to a routine schedule but rather based on issues that represent the greatest risks to investor protection and market integrity.

OCIE has not inspected FINRA's fixed-income surveillance programs or MSRB since 2005. OCIE's inspections of FINRA and MSRB in 2005 produced findings related to their municipal securities oversight activities.[74] While the two SROs responded to OCIE's findings and recommendations with corrective actions or, in a few cases, rebuttals, OCIE has not yet confirmed through on-site inspections whether they have adequately addressed these recommendations. OCIE staff only recently began a new inspection of FINRA that will encompass its fixed-income surveillance program, including the municipal trade reporting and markup reviews. OCIE has not yet begun another inspection of MSRB.

OCIE staff said that staffing constraints had prevented them from starting another inspection sooner to review FINRA's fixed-income surveillance program and MSRB.

According to OCIE data, staffing of OCIE's Market Oversight group, which is responsible for inspections of FINRA and MSRB and other SROs that are not clearing agencies, has declined by 5 employees (about 12 percent) since fiscal year 2007—when we last reported on staffing of this group—and by 24 employees (nearly 40 percent) since fiscal year 2005. [75] As shown in table 5, as of September 2011, the Market Oversight group consisted of 38 active staff, including 12 managers, 25 professional staff (examiners), and 1 support staff. According to OCIE staff, the majority of staff members in the Market Oversight group have a law degree, and 11 people have prior experience in fixed-income issues.

Furthermore, OCIE staff stated that positions in the Market Oversight group are a mixture of entry-level and senior positions, with staff typically staying approximately 4 to 5 years before going elsewhere within or outside of SEC.

As of September 2011, according to OCIE staff, the Market Oversight group had seven vacant slots, but an SEC hiring freeze limited OCIE's ability to fill most of these positions.

Table 5. Number of OCIE Market Oversight Staff, Fiscal Years 2005-2011

	Managers			Staff		
Fiscal year	*Senior officer*	*Assistant director*	*Branch chief*	*Professional*[a]	*Support*	*Year total*
2005	2	4	9	43	4	62
2006	2	3	9	29	4	47
2007	2	4	8	26	3	43
2008	2	4	8	35	2	51
2009	2	3	8	34	2	49
2010	1	4	8	33	1	47
2011 (as of 9/16/2011)	1	4	7	25	1	38

Source: GAO summary of OCIE data.

[a] According to the information OCIE provided, there were 27 professional staff in the group as of September 16, 2011. However, that number includes two people who were detailed to other offices in the agency and were not actively working in the Market Oversight group. Therefore, we list the number of available professional staff as 25 rather than 27.

Although OCIE is transitioning to a risk-based approach to SRO inspections, it lacks sufficient data on the SROs' fixed-income regulatory activities that it could use to inform this approach. OCIE's mission includes protecting investors and ensuring market integrity through risk-based strategies that, among other things, are designed to improve compliance and monitor risk. However, OCIE currently engages in limited monitoring of the SROs between inspections and may not have sufficient sources of information to allow it to effectively assess the risk level of SROs' regulatory programs. OCIE staff told us that they plan to convene all of the SROs in early 2012 to, among other things, clarify expectations relating to their activities. One of the objectives of the SRO outreach will be to share issues that OCIE identified in assessments it conducted of all equity and options SROs in 2011 that have implications across the SROs. However, this effort will not provide staff with information on the quality of ongoing SRO oversight in any particular area—such as fixed-income surveillance—between inspections. OCIE staff also participate in the meetings mandated by the Dodd-Frank Act that include SEC, MSRB, and FINRA. While such communication is essential to helping ensure uniform interpretation of MSRB rules and discussing recent trends in enforcement, among other things, it does not provide insight into the ongoing effectiveness of SRO regulatory programs. We found that OCIE received and reviewed quarterly reports from FINRA on its regulatory activities related to municipal securities markups and markdowns. However, an OCIE staff member told us that the reports, which present aggregate statistics, reveal little about the effectiveness of FINRA's activities in this area.

For a risk-based inspection approach to be effective, it is essential for OCIE to maintain ongoing monitoring and communication with the SROs to keep abreast of the current operations and to use this information to update its supervisory strategies. We note that the review period OCIE covered in its 2005 FINRA inspection predated the recent financial crisis and ensuing volatility in the municipal securities market. Although OCIE is now conducting an inspection of FINRA that encompasses its fixed-income surveillance program, it had not obtained any information since its last inspection about the quality of FINRA's market oversight. Further, MSRB implemented RTRS in 2005 and began making real-time trade price information freely and publicly available on the EMMA website in 2008, but OCIE has not performed any independent reviews or otherwise obtained information to establish the quality or reliability of the data in this system, despite the fact that market participants use it for pricing purposes and that SEC, FINRA, and the federal banking regulators rely heavily on the data to carry out their regulatory activities.[76]

SEC proposed a rule (17a-26) in 2004 that would require certain SROs (specifically, national securities exchanges or registered securities associations, such as FINRA) to periodically review the operation and performance of their regulatory programs. This rule was intended to allow OCIE to monitor the SROs covered by the rule during the periods between inspections and identify both SRO-specific issues as well as common issues across multiple SROs. The rule would, among other things, require SROs it covered to submit quarterly reports to SEC on the results of their regulatory activities, including surveillance, complaints received, and investigations, examinations, and enforcement actions.[77] While the proposed rule in its current form may have some limitations— for example, the quarterly reports might not provide OCIE with much insight into the effectiveness of the SROs' regulatory activities—it would provide a mechanism for OCIE to regularly collect and analyze information from the SROs. Without collecting information on an ongoing basis that provides insight into the effectiveness of SRO regulatory programs, OCIE may not be able to identify anomalies or changes in the operations that warrant more immediate inspections.

CONCLUSION

OCIE is transitioning to a risk-based approach for its SRO inspection program and is convening a meeting with the SROs in 2012 to share issues staff have already identified that have implications across the SROs. Among other things, the risk-based approach is intended to improve compliance and monitor risk.

While OCIE's efforts to implement a risk-based inspection program have the potential to better target scarce resources to high-risk areas, its limited monitoring of the SROs between inspections could result in its missing potential new or ongoing issues with their regulatory programs. For example, OCIE's last inspection of FINRA's fixed-income surveillance program predated the recent financial crisis and ensuing volatility in the municipal securities markets.

Although OCIE obtained some information on FINRA's examination program through its district office inspections and broker-dealer examinations, its lack of a structured mechanism for monitoring the quality of FINRA's fixed-income surveillance during that time means that OCIE will not have a full picture of how effective FINRA was in surveilling for and detecting violations of MSRB rules until it finishes its 2011 inspection—more than 3 years after the financial crisis began and more than 6 years since its last inspection.

Proposed Rule 17a-26 is an example of a mechanism that OCIE could use to obtain meaningful information for ongoing monitoring of SRO regulatory programs for the municipal securities market. This proposed rule would compel the SROs to review, on an annual and a quarterly basis, the operation and performance of their regulatory programs and report the results of these reviews to SEC.

Finalizing this rule—revised as necessary to reflect OCIE's current informational needs—would allow OCIE examiners to formally collect and analyze interim data on the operation and effectiveness of SROs' programs and potentially facilitate ongoing oversight of SROs between inspections. Such information could provide regulators with more up-to-date information on the state of the market and SROs' regulatory efforts. In addition, it could help OCIE meet its goal of identifying high-risk areas and leverage its staff resources appropriately. Unless OCIE takes steps to gather and analyze information on the SROs' fixed-income regulatory programs on an ongoing basis, it may not learn about emerging or recurring issues or risks in a timely manner and take steps to address them.

RECOMMENDATION FOR EXECUTIVE ACTION

To improve SEC's ability to monitor the operations and effectiveness of SRO regulatory programs related to municipal securities trading between inspections and to help identify areas of high risk, we recommend that the Chairman of the Securities and Exchange Commission direct OCIE to take steps to gather and analyze information on the SROs' fixed-income regulatory programs on an ongoing basis and use it to inform their risk-based inspection approach.

AGENCY COMMENTS AND OUR EVALUATION

We provided a draft of this report for comment to the SEC Chairman for her review and comment. SEC provided written comments. SEC also provided technical comments that were incorporated as appropriate. In addition, we provided a draft of this report to the Federal Reserve, FDIC, and OCC, for their review and comment. These agencies did not provide written comments, but we incorporated their technical comments where appropriate. We also provided a copy of the draft report to MSRB and FINRA for their review and incorporated technical comments from them as appropriate.

In its written comments, SEC agreed with our findings. With respect to our recommendation that SEC improve its ability to monitor the operations and effectiveness of SRO regulatory programs between inspections by gathering and analyzing information from the SROs on an ongoing basis, SEC agreed that more enhanced oversight of the SROs' fixed-income regulatory programs is needed and that it has already begun that process through the transition to a risk-focused approach. SEC noted, however, that more frequent review and analysis would require additional staff resources and reiterated that OCIE has been unable to fill several vacant positions in its Market Oversight group due to limitations on SEC hiring under a Continuing Resolution. SEC further noted that even if the vacant positions were filled, OCIE's Market Oversight group would continue to be understaffed relative to the number and complexity of entities that it examines and that it would need additional resources to conduct more frequent inspections of FINRA and MSRB's fixed-income programs or to do interim monitoring of FINRA's fixed income surveillance program. As we observed, SEC's efforts to implement a risk-based inspection program have the potential to better target its scarce resources to high-risk areas. Gathering and analyzing data from the SROs on an ongoing basis could help SEC better meet its goal of identifying high-risk areas and leveraging its staff resources for inspections.

A. Nicole Clowers Director
Financial Markets and Community Investment

APPENDIX I. POTENTIAL USES, RISKS, AND OVERSIGHT OF DERIVATIVE PRODUCTS IN THE MUNICIPAL SECURITIES MARKET

Prior to the financial crisis that began in the summer of 2007, municipal governments made increasing use of interest rate swaps, a derivative product.[1] In an interest rate swap, a municipal issuer enters into a contract with a counterparty (typically an investment bank, commercial bank, or insurance company), and agrees to exchange periodic interest payments. Municipal issuers may use interest rate swaps to try to lower their borrowing costs. For example, by issuing variable-rate securities and entering into a variable-to-fixed interest rate swap, an issuer may be able to obtain a lower fixed-rate interest payment than it otherwise could obtain if it had issued fixed-rate securities directly. In this case, after issuing the variable-rate securities, the issuer enters into a swap agreement with a counterparty that agrees to pay the issuer a variable rate based on an index that is intended to approximate the variable-rate interest payments that the issuer must make to its investors. In exchange, the issuer agrees to pay the counterparty a fixed interest rate. As a result, the issuer achieves a synthetic fixed rate by converting a variable-rate obligation to a fixed-rate obligation.[2] Payment exchanges between the issuer and the counterparty reflect differences between the fixed rate and the variable rate during a specific period of time. The swap does not alter the issuer's obligations, including debt servicing, to existing investors.[3]

Municipal issuers incur a number of risks when they enter into interest rate swaps, including basis risk, termination risk, and counterparty risk Basis risk is the risk that the variable rate paid by the issuer to its investors is more than the variable interest rate received under the swap. If that occurs, the payments the issuer receives from the counterparty are less than the payments the issuer must make to the investors. The issuer must cover that difference in addition to paying the fixed rate on the swap to the counterparty. Termination risk is the risk that the swap may terminate or be terminated before its expiration. Swap agreements allow for termination of the swap by either party in the case of certain events, such as payment defaults on the swap or credit rating downgrades. For example, if the issuer triggers an early termination, it could owe a termination payment reflecting the value of the swap under the market conditions at that time. If market rates have changed to the issuer's disadvantage (e.g., the issuer is a fixed-rate payer and interest rates have declined), the issuer will be "out of the money" on the swap, that is, the fixed rate that the issuer is paying to the counterparty is higher than the current market rate, and owe the counterparty a termination payment. A termination of a swap can result in a substantial unexpected payment obligation. Counterparty risk is the risk that the counterparty will default on its payment obligations to the issuer.

The recent financial crisis heightened the exposure of a number of municipal issuers with interest rate swaps to these risks. For example, a number of municipal issuers had insured their underlying variable-rate securities with bond insurance. However, the downgrades in these insurers' credit ratings during the financial crisis resulted in some issuers having to post collateral on the swap agreements they had entered into or face termination of the swaps.[4] Because interest rates had declined significantly at that time, these issuers were out of the money—making it expensive to terminate the contract. However, a number of issuers refunded their variable rate securities and terminated the swaps to free themselves from these agreements.

In some cases where municipal issuers have suffered losses because of swap agreements, issuers allege that the counterparties that sold them the swaps (swap dealers) misrepresented the risks of the swaps that they sold to the issuers. In other cases, they have called into question the fees that the swap dealers made. Questions grew that some of the municipal issuers that entered into swaps during this period did not understand these complicated products or their risks.

Pursuant to the Dodd-Frank Act, CFTC Has Issued Rules Regulating Swap Dealers' Transactions with Municipal Issuers

Title VII of the Dodd-Frank Wall Street Reform and Consumer Protection Act (Dodd-Frank Act) created a comprehensive framework to provide oversight over the previously unregulated over-the counter derivatives market. The Dodd-Frank Act provided the Commodities Futures Trading Commission

(CFTC) the authority to regulate swaps, including interest rate swaps.[5] Section 731 specifically amended the Commodity Exchange Act (CEA) to provide CFTC with both mandatory and discretionary rulemaking authority to impose business conduct requirements on swap dealers and major swap participants in their dealings with counterparties generally, including municipal issuers, which are among the entities termed "special entities."[6] In January 2012, CFTC issued rules to implement this authority.[7]

Among other things, the rules establish a "know your counterparty" requirement. This requirement requires a swap dealer (but not a major swap participant) that acts as an adviser to a special entity to make a reasonable determination that any swap it recommends is in the special entity's best interest and make reasonable efforts to obtain information necessary to make a reasonable determination that the swap it recommends is in the special entity's best interest.[8] The swap dealer will comply with its duty to act in the special entity's best interest where it complies with the "reasonable efforts" requirement, acts in good faith and makes full and fair disclosure of all material facts and conflicts of interest with respect to the recommended swap, and employs reasonable care that the swap is designed to further the special entity's objectives. The rules also require swap dealers and major swap participants to disclose to their counterparties material information about swaps, including material risks, characteristics, incentives, and conflicts of interest. Additionally, CFTC's rules establish several duties for swap dealer and major swap participants, including the duty to verify a counterparty's eligibility to transact in the swap markets, provide the daily midmarket value of uncleared swaps to the counterparty, and ensure all communications to the counterparty are fair and balanced. A swap dealer who recommends a swap must conduct reasonable diligence to understand risks and rewards of the recommendation and have a reasonable basis to believe that the recommendation is suitable for the counterparty.

The rules also establish a duty for any swap dealer that acts as an adviser to a special entity to act in its best interests, which includes recommending a swap or trading strategy involving a swap.[9] The rules establish a duty for swap dealers and major swap participants to have a reasonable basis to believe that any special entity counterparty has a representative that meets the following criteria:

- is sufficiently knowledgeable to evaluate the transaction and risks;
- is not subject to statutory disqualification;
- is independent of the swap dealer or major swap participant;

- undertakes a duty to act in the best interests of the special entity;
- makes appropriate and timely disclosures to the special entity;
- evaluates, consistent with any guidelines provided by the special entity, fair pricing and appropriateness of the swap;
- in the case of a special entity that is an employee benefit plan subject to the Employee Retirement Income Security Act of 1974 (ERISA), is a fiduciary as defined in Section 3 of ERISA; and
- in the case of a special entity that is a municipal entity, is subject to restrictions on certain political contributions to certain public officials of the municipal entity.

For special entities other than employee benefit plans subject to ERISA, the final rule provides a safe harbor under which the swap dealer will be deemed to have a reasonable basis to believe that the special entity has a qualified representative if the certain conditions are met, including the representative stating in writing that it has policies and procedures designed to ensure that it satisfies the applicable criteria.

Appendix II. Scope and Methodology

To analyze how institutional and individual investors trade municipal securities in the secondary market and the factors affecting the prices institutional and individual investors receive, we obtained data on all municipal securities trades that broker-dealers reported to the Municipal Securities Rulemaking Board's (MSRB) Real-Time Transaction Reporting System (RTRS) from January 1, 2005, to December 31, 2010.[1] For each trade, the data included variables describing characteristics of the security, including the dated date (the date from which interest starts to accrue), maturity date, interest rate, principal amount at issuance, and reoffering price (the price at which underwriters sell newly issued securities to the public in the primary market), as well as variables describing the characteristics of the trade (trade date/time, settlement date, trade price, yield, and trade amount) and trade type (dealer sales to customer, interdealer trade, or dealer purchases from customer). We analyzed trade data involving newly issued fixed-rate securities to understand how trade prices differ for institutional and individual investors, using trade size (amount) as a proxy for whether the trade involved institutional or individual investors.[2] We focused on trades that occurred within the period from 30 days prior to and 120 days after the dated date on municipal securities.[3] We chose to examine this time frame because we observed that bonds in our sample trade most frequently around the time of issuance and that trading activity declines as the number of days after issuance increases, with trading activity typically leveling off by about 120 days after issuance. Focusing on a period with more trading activity improved the precision with which we measured the relationships described below. We chose to examine only trades of newly issued bonds to ensure that all the trades we analyzed involved bonds that had been available to investors for a similar amount of time and to limit the likelihood that unobserved, time-varying characteristics of bonds influence our analysis.

First, we analyzed the relationship between the relative trade price (the trade price as a percentage of the reoffering price) and trade amount by trade type in order to determine if prices for smaller trades—those more likely to involve individual investors—are different from prices for larger trades—those that are more likely to involve institutional investors. Second, we analyzed the relationships between spreads (the difference between the price on dealer sales to investors and the price on dealer purchases from investors as a percentage of the price on dealer purchases) within $10,000 trade amount increments and trade amount to determine if spreads on smaller trades are different from spreads on larger trades. For these regressions, we constructed datasets with one observation for each security for each $10,000 trade amount increment. For each security, for each $10,000 trade amount increment, we calculated the inside spread, mean spread, and outside spread. The inside spread is the difference between the lowest trade price on a dealer sale and the highest trade price on a dealer purchase as a percentage of the highest trade price on a dealer purchase. The mean spread is the difference between the mean trade price on a dealer sale and the mean trade price on a dealer purchase as a percentage of the mean trade price on a dealer purchase. The outside spread is the difference between the highest trade price on a dealer sale and the lowest trade price on a dealer purchase as a percentage of the lowest trade price on a dealer purchase. We only used observations on security-trade amount increment combinations for which there existed at least one dealer sale and at least one dealer purchase. Third, we analyzed the relationship between price dispersion (the difference between the maximum and minimum trade price as a percentage of average trade price) and trade amount by trade type to determine if prices on smaller trades are more or less dispersed than prices on larger trades. For these regressions, we constructed datasets with one observation for each security, for each trade type, and for each trade amount in $10,000 increments. We formed groups of trades for each security, trade type, and trade amount in $10,000 increments. We then calculated price dispersion for that group of trades as the difference between the maximum trade price and minimum trade price as a percentage of the average trade price. For all three analyses, our regressions included indicator variables for each security in the sample to control for unobserved, time-invariant features of the securities. We estimated separate regressions for bonds issued in each year from 2005 through 2010. We present the results of our regression analyses in appendix III.

For illustrative purposes, we also calculated descriptive statistics using the trade data. First, we calculated the average relative trade price on newly issued fixed-rate securities by trade amount and trade type for 2010. Second, we determined the average spreads for a $20,000 trade (an individual investor-sized trade) and a $5 million trade (a institutional investor-sized trade) of a fixed-rate security in 2010. We then used these average spreads to calculate the yield to maturity of two hypothetical trades of $20,000 and $5 million of the same security. We did this to compare the effect of the size of the spread on the return received by an individual investor and an institutional investor. Third, we calculated the average price dispersion for newly issued fixed-rate securities by trade amount and trade type for 2010. We presented these descriptive statistics in tables in the report. In conducting our analyses, we carried out a data reliability assessment of the MSRB trade data. To do so, we reviewed information on the processes and procedures MSRB uses to help ensure that trade data entered into RTRS are accurate and complete. We also reviewed the data for missing values and outliers and, where we observed instances of such, solicited explanations from MSRB staff. On the basis of this information, we determined that these data were reliable for our purposes.

We also obtained statistics on the relative size of the municipal securities market. We obtained data from the Federal Reserve's Flow of Funds Accounts of the United States on the estimated dollar value of municipal securities outstanding and from Bloomberg L.P. (Bloomberg) on the number of municipal issuers and outstanding municipal securities that it tracks. We also collected data on the total number of public companies listed on the major U.S. exchanges from the annual reports of NYSE Euronext and NASDAQ OMX. We did not conduct an assessment of the reliability of these data sources. However, these data are widely used by regulators, market professionals, and academics and are considered credible for the purposes for which we used them. In addition, we used these data solely for descriptive purposes and not for the purpose of making recommendations or drawing conclusions about causality.

We reviewed studies that analyzed pricing in the municipal securities market. We limited our survey to those studies using data from 1995 or later. We did this because prior to 1995, there was no systematic and comprehensive dissemination of post-trade information for municipal securities. We identified five relevant studies by searching the EconLit, the JSTOR, the National Bureau of Economic Research (NBER) Working Paper Series, and the Social Science Research Network (SSRN) databases.[4] We identified two additional studies through our interviews with market participants. Although we did not identify methodological concerns with these studies, the inclusion of these studies is for research purposes and does not imply that we deem them to be definitive. In addition, we attended or viewed the Securities and Exchange Commission's (SEC) field hearings on the state of the municipal securities market, reviewed industry literature, and interviewed members of trade organizations representing institutional investors, broker-dealers (including broker's brokers), and individual investors; academics; SEC Office of Municipal Securities Market officials; MSRB officials and independent municipal market research and advisory firms. We also reviewed information from these entities on the availability of pre- and post-trade pricing information in the marketplace, and we spoke to market participants interested in forming an exchange for municipal securities. To understand how electronic systems and trading platforms are used in the trading of municipal securities, we received a demonstration from Bloomberg on the services it offers to municipal broker-dealers and other subscribers to facilitate municipal securities trading and analysis. We also reviewed existing alternative trading systems (ATS) operating in this market by analyzing their annual Form ATSs submitted to SEC and other descriptive information and received a demonstration from one ATS of its electronic platform for trading municipal securities.

To determine how federal regulators enforce MSRB rules to ensure fair and reasonable prices for investors and the timely and accurate reporting of municipal trades, we reviewed relevant MSRB rules, guidance, and proposed rules. We focused on Rules G-30, G-14, G-12, and G-15, which address pricing, trade reporting, and trade clearance and settlement. We also reviewed documentation describing RegWeb, the web portal MSRB makes available to federal regulators to analyze and query RTRS data for regulatory purposes; the Financial Industry Regulatory Authority's (FINRA) policies and procedures for electronically surveilling RTRS data for potential violations of MSRB pricing and trade reporting rules; and FINRA and federal banking regulators' (Office of the Comptroller of the Currency, or OCC; Federal Deposit

Insurance Corporation, or FDIC; and Board of Governors of the Federal Reserve System, or the Federal Reserve) examination procedures for assessing broker-dealer compliance with these rules.

We also identified enforcement trends related to Rules G-14 and G-30. With respect to FINRA, we reviewed results of the periodic surveillance of trade data it conducted from 2006 to 2010 to monitor broker-dealers and bank dealers for potential violations of MSRB Rules G-14 and G-30. These results included the number of alerts FINRA's surveillance programs generated on potential G-14 and G-30 violations, as well as the resolution (for example, no further review, cautionary action, etc.) of each alert. We also reviewed data from FINRA's System for Tracking Activities for Regulatory Policy and Oversight (STAR), which tracks the life cycle of FINRA's regulatory matters, on the number of municipal-related broker-dealer examinations FINRA conducted from 2006 to 2010, the number of those examinations that identified violations of MSRB Rules G-14 and G30, and the resolution of each examination. We conducted a reliability assessment of the FINRA data and determined they were reliable for our purpose. Specifically, we reviewed information on the STAR system and FINRA's policies and procedures for ensuring the data entered into the STAR system were accurate and complete.

We reviewed a purposeful sample of 45 examinations FINRA conducted from 2006 to 2010 in which it identified violations of MSRB Rules G-14 and G-30. We reviewed these examinations to inform our understanding of how FINRA examiners applied their policies and procedures for assessing compliance with Rules G-14 and G-30. First, we selected all 11 examinations that had both G-14 and G-30 violations. Next, we selected an additional 6 examinations with G-30 violations that were forwarded to other agencies (such as SEC) for further review or initiated for a specific cause, as opposed to routine examinations. Third, 8 examinations with G-30 violations were selected systematically by selecting every 4th examination after ordering the remaining examinations with G-30 violations by the completion date. Finally, we similarly selected 20 additional examinations with G-14 violations by selecting every 20th examination from an ordered listing of remaining examinations with G-14 violations.[5] We did not extrapolate the information in the sample examinations to the universe of municipal broker-dealer examinations. Rather, we drew examples from some of the examinations to illustrate concepts in the report.

With respect to federal banking regulators' enforcement of Rules G-14 and G-30, we reviewed data on the number of bank dealer examinations each regulator conducted from 2006 to 2010 and the number of those examinations that identified violations of Rules G-14 and G-30, among other MSRB rules. We conducted a reliability assessment of the federal banking regulator data and determined they were reliable for our purpose. Specifically, we reviewed information from federal banking regulators on the systems from which they generated the data provided to us and their policies and procedures for ensuring the data were accurate and complete. From the examination data, we selected and reviewed examinations or their relevant excerpts to observe examples of cases in which the federal banking regulators identified violations of Rule G-14 or other MSRB rules.[6] As with the FINRA examinations, we reviewed these examinations to inform our understanding of how federal banking examiners applied their policies and procedures for assessing compliance with Rules G-14 and G-30. We did not extrapolate the information to the universe of bank dealer examinations.

We also identified trends in the incidences of late reporting of transactions (i.e., reported more than 15 minutes after the time of trade) by broker-dealers to the RTRS since its implementation in 2005. More specifically, we analyzed data on the number of late-reported trades MSRB identified each month from January 2005 to July 2011 and the total trades reported for those months. In reviewing these data, we carried out a data reliability assessment. To do so, we reviewed information on the processes and procedures MSRB uses to identify late trades in RTRS. We determined these data were reliable for our purposes.

To identify trends in settlement failures in municipal securities transactions, we reviewed data from the National Securities Clearing Corporation (NSCC). This self-regulatory organization (SRO) provides clearance and settlement services for a variety of securities, including equity, corporate, and municipal securities. Because NSCC typically does not track settlement failures by security type, we requested that NSCC perform a specialized query to provide us with this information. NSCC reviewed a 5- day trading period, from June 6 to June 10, 2011, and provided us with the dollar value of municipal securities settlement failures, as well as the total dollar value of all settlement failures, for that period. We did not assess the reliability of these data because we used the data solely for descriptive purposes and not for the purpose of making recommendations or drawing conclusions about causality. However, we corroborated the data by asking regulators and market participants about their experience with municipal trade failures, and what they told us was consistent with the trends in the data.

To understand how SEC oversees the municipal market, we reviewed the SEC Office of Compliance Inspections and Examinations' (OCIE) guidance for conducting oversight inspections of FINRA-registered broker-dealers, focusing on policies and procedures for assessing compliance with MSRB rules related to pricing and trade reporting, and we reviewed OCIE's guidance for conducting inspections of SROs. We reviewed data from OCIE on broker-dealer examinations it conducted from 2002 to 2010 that assessed compliance with municipal securities rules and regulations, including information on the MSRB rule violations examiners identified. We conducted a reliability assessment of these data and determined that there were limitations to how we could use them. We reviewed information on OCIE's system for tracking examination data (the Super Tracking and Reporting System, or STARS), reviewed OCIE's policies and procedures for ensuring the completeness and accuracy of the data, and interviewed OCIE officials. Although we determined that STARS data are reliable, we learned that STARS does not contain a unique field that allows users to retrieve all examinations with a municipal component. Rather, OCIE officials ran a report by searching for key words that, based on their experience with STARS data, were likely to be included in an examination with a municipal component. This produced a list of approximately 1,100 examinations conducted from 2002 to 2010. We determined this was a reasonable way to proceed to identify a significant portion of the targeted universe of examinations from which we would draw selected exams for our review.

We reviewed a purposeful sample of 35 examinations that OCIE conducted from 2002 to 2010 in which it identified violations of MSRB Rules G-14 and G-30. First, we selected all 13 examinations that had G30 violations. Four of these examinations also had G-14 violations. We then selected an additional 22 examinations with G-14 violations (from a total of 80 examinations with G-14 violations during the time period). For the latter group, we attempted to select examinations representing the entire time period and a variety of recommended actions (from minor deficiency letters to enforcement referrals). We reviewed the examinations to understand how OCIE examiners applied OCIE's examination policies and procedures to assess broker-dealers for compliance with MSRB rules. However, we did not cite any OCIE examination statistics in the report, given that the list of 1,100 examinations may not have included all municipal examinations OCIE conducted from 2002 to 2010, as well as the fact that OCIE uses a risk-based method and does not necessarily review for broker-dealer compliance with Rules G-30 and G-14 in every examination.[7] We also reviewed OCIE's 2002 and 2005 inspections of MSRB and FINRA's fixed-income program, focusing on OCIE's review of FINRA's surveillance, examination, and enforcement programs for overseeing municipal securities trading.[8] In addition, we reviewed MSRB's and FINRA's responses to OCIE's inspection reports. Finally we reviewed OCIE's inspections of FINRA's district offices from 2000 to 2010 and its 2009 inspections of the Depository Trust Company and NSCC, SROs that clear and settle municipal securities transactions.

We also reviewed meeting minutes, e-mails, training presentations, MSRB's memorandum of understanding with FINRA, and other relevant documentation from MSRB to understand the coordination among SEC, MSRB, FINRA, and federal banking regulators in conducting oversight of the municipal securities market. Finally, we interviewed officials from OCIE, Office of Municipal Securities, SEC's Division of Enforcement, MSRB, FINRA, and federal banking regulators to better understand their oversight of the municipal securities market and efforts to coordinate their oversight activities.

We conducted this performance audit from November 2010 to January 2012 in accordance with generally accepted government auditing standards. Those standards require that we plan and perform the audit to obtain sufficient, appropriate evidence to provide a reasonable basis for our findings and conclusions based on our audit objectives.

APPENDIX III. GAO ANALYSIS OF MSRB TRADE DATA, 2005-2010

To understand how trade prices for individual investors differ from those for institutional investors, we analyzed trade data on newly issued fixed-rate municipal securities from the Municipal Securities Rulemaking Board's Real-Time Trade Reporting System from January 1, 2005, through December 31, 2010, using trade size as a proxy for whether the trade involved institutional or individual investors.[1] We focused on trades that occurred within the period from 30 days prior to and 120 days after the dated date on municipal securities. We chose to examine this time frame because we observed that (1) securities in our sample trade most frequently around the time of issuance, (2) trading activity declines within days after issuance, and (3) trading activity has typically leveled off by about 120 days after issuance. Focusing on a period with more trading activity improves the precision with which we measure the relationships described below.[2] We chose to examine only trades of newly issued bonds to ensure that all the trades we analyzed involved bonds that had been available to investors for a similar amount of time and to limit the likelihood that unobserved, time-varying characteristics of bonds influence our analysis.

First, we analyzed how relative prices—defined as trade prices as a percentage of the reoffering prices (the prices at which the securities were originally sold to the public by the underwriter)—changed as trade size increased for different types of trades (dealer sales to investors and dealer purchases from investors). To do so, we estimated regressions on security trades. The dependent variables in these regressions are the relative price of a trade, and the independent variables in these regressions are trade amount interacted with trade type and indicator variables for each security in the sample. The security indicators control for time-invariant features of a security that may affect the relative price at which it trades. We estimated separate regressions for securities issued in each year from 2005 through 2010. We present our regression results in table 6. Our analysis shows that, relative to institutional investors, individual investors generally pay higher prices when buying—and receive lower prices when selling—municipal securities.

- Relative prices at which broker-dealers sold securities to investors declined on average with trade amount for all years in the analysis. For all years, this negative relationship is statistically significant at the 1 percent level.
- Relative prices at which broker-dealers purchased securities from investors increased with trade amount for bonds issued in every year except 2009. For every year except 2009, this positive relationship is statistically significant at the 1 percent level. For 2009, this relationship is negative but it is not statistically significant from zero.

Second, we analyzed how broker-dealers' spreads—defined as the difference between the price on dealer sales to investors and the price on dealer purchases from investors as a percentage of the price on dealer purchases—changed as trade size increased, using three different measures of spread. For this analysis, we estimated regressions on securities. The dependent variables in these regressions are the spread on a security over a $10,000 trade amount increment, and the independent variables in these regressions are trade amount and indicator variables for each security in the sample. The security indicators control for time-invariant features of a security that may affect its spread. We estimated separate regressions for securities issued in each year from 2005 through 2010. We present our regression results in table 7. Our analysis showed, on average, broker-dealers receive larger spreads when trading smaller blocks of municipal securities. For all years and for all three measures of spread, this relationship is statistically significant at the 1 percent level.

Table 6. Percentage Change in Relative Price per 1 Percent Change in Trade Amount, by Trade Type and Year, 2005-2010

Year	Broker-dealer sales to investors	Broker-dealer purchasesfrom investors
2005	-0.0017%	0.0018%
	[73.64][a]	[24.94]
2006	-0.0020%	0.0011%
	[79.39]	[18.21]
2007	-0.0018%	0.0016%
	[62.49]	[21.64]
2008	-0.0015%	0.0033%
	[24.09]	[14.88]
2009	-0.0022%	-0.0003%
	[44.39]	[1.60]
2010	-0.0020%	0.0010%
	[48.94]	[7.99]

Source: GAO analysis of data from MSRB.

[a]Brackets contain t-statistics calculated using standard errors that are adjusted for heteroskedasticity and for within-bond correlation. For all years, the relationship between relative trade price and trade amount is negative for dealer sales to customers, and the negative relationship is statistically significant at the 1 percent level. For every year except 2009, the relationship between relative trade price and trade amount is positive for dealer purchases from customers, and the positive relationship is statistically significant at the 1 percent level. For 2009, the relationship between relative trade price and trade amount is negative for dealer purchases from customers, but it is not statistically significantly different from zero. For all years and for all trade types, the relationship between price dispersion and trade amount is negative, and the negative relationship is statistically significant at the 1 percent level.

- The inside spread, which estimated a lower bound for broker-dealer spreads, declined as trade size increased for all years in the analysis.[3]

- The mean spread, which estimated average broker-dealer spreads, declined as trade size increased for all years in the analysis.[4]
- The outside spread, which estimated an upper bound for broker-dealer spreads, declined as trade size increased for all years in the analysis.[5]

Table 7. Percentage Change in Spread per $10,000 Increase in Trade Amount, by Year, 2005-2010

Year	Inside spread	Mean spread	Outside spread
2005	-0.22%	-0.29%	-0.33%
	[8.73] [a]	[14.50]	[17.77]
2006	-0.19%	-0.23%	-0.25%
	[9.71]	[13.43]	[17.06]
2007	-0.16%	-0.19%	-0.20%
	[9.51]	[13.68]	[18.31]
2008	-0.23%	-0.33%	-0.47%
	[8.12]	[13.31]	[22.16]
2009	-0.31%	-0.41%	-0.53%
	[10.45]	[19.52]	[30.38]
2010	-0.35%	-0.42%	-0.47%
	[14.72]	[20.34]	[29.26]

Source: GAO analysis of data from MSRB.

[a] Brackets contain the absolute values of t-statistics calculated using standard errors that are adjusted for heteroskedasticity and for within-bond correlation. For all years and for all three measures of spread, the relationship between spread and trade amount is negative, and the negative relationship is statistically significant at the 1 percent level.

Third, we analyzed how price dispersion, defined as the difference between the maximum and minimum trade price as a percentage of average trade price, changed as trade size increased. For this analysis, we again estimated regressions on securities.

The dependent variables in these regressions are the price dispersion over a $10,000 trade amount increment, and the independent variables in these regressions are trade amount interacted with trade type and indicator variables for each security in the sample.

The security indicators control for time-invariant features of a security that may affect its price dispersion. We estimated separate regressions for securities issued in each year from 2005 through 2010. See table 8 for the regression results.

Our analysis showed that prices for larger trades tended to be more concentrated, while prices for smaller trades tended to be more dispersed. For all years, this relationship is statistically significant at the 1 percent level.

- For broker-dealer sales to investors, the measure of dispersion declined as trade amount increased.

For broker-dealer purchases from investors, the measure of dispersion also declined as trade amount increased.

Table 8. Change in Price Dispersion per $10,000 Increase in Trade Amount (in Basis Points), by Trade Type and Year, 2005-2010

Year	Broker-dealer sales to investors	Broker-dealer purchases frominvestors
2005	-0.14%	-0.04%
	[45.64][a]	[11.53]
2006	-0.11%	-0.03%
	[47.53]	[11.11]
2007	-0.13%	-0.04%
	[38.02]	[9.74]
2008	-0.41%	-0.26%
	[52.39]	[18.54]
2009	-0.39%	-0.19%
	[65.81]	[14.60]
2010	-0.33%	-0.15%
	[68.79]	[17.96]

Source: GAO analysis of data from MSRB.

[a] Brackets contain the absolute values of t-statistics calculated using standard errors that are adjusted for heteroskedasticity and for within-bond correlation. For all years and for all trade types, the relationship between price dispersion and trade amount is negative, and the negative relationship is statistically significant at the 1 percent level.

APPENDIX IV. MUNICIPAL SECURITIES RULEMAKING BOARD EXPENSES AND REVENUES RELATED TO THE MARKET INFORMATION TRANSPARENCY PROGRAMS

The Municipal Securities Rulemaking Board intends for its Market Information Transparency Programs (Transparency Programs) to protect investors by fostering availabilty and transparency of critical information about municipal securities and market activity. From fiscal years 2004 through 2010, MSRB spent significant resources developing and operating these programs. MSRB's total revenue has fluctuated during this period. To generate additional revenues to continue to enhance and maintain these transparency programs, in fiscal year 2010 MSRB increased transaction fees for broker-dealers and imposed a new technology fee.

MSRB's Transparency Programs Make Municipal Data and Documents Publicly Available

MSRB currently implements five transparency programs that coordinate the collection and dissemination of specific market information.

- *Primary Market Disclosure Program:* manages official statements and other primary market documents about new issues of municipal securities.
- *Continuing Disclosure Program:* manages ongoing disclosures about existing municipal securities.
- *Transaction Data Program:* collects and disseminates real-time municipal trade price information.
- *Short-Term Disclosure Program:* manages interest rate and related information about auction rate securities and variable rate demand obligations.
- *Political Contribution Disclosure Program:* manages quarterly reports of political contributions and municipal securities business from municipal securities dealers active in the new issue market in connection with MSRB Rule G-37.[1]

MSRB makes available most data and documents it collects to the public at no charge on its Electronic Municipal Market Access (EMMA) website.[2]

MSRB launched the EMMA website in 2008.[3] The EMMA website makes trade prices available on a real-time basis along with historical market trading information dating back to January 31, 2005, and issuer's continuing disclosure documents are available for disclosures posted to the EMMA website beginning in July 2009. New issue disclosure documents are available for issues dating back to 1990. The EMMA website also provides information on the market and investor educational material and offering documents for municipal fund securities.

MSRB staff told us that they are developing a 5-year plan that will guide future enhancements to the EMMA website. In doing so, they said they will consider what improvements would make the EMMA website more meaningful and useful, how MSRB can help individual investors understand what information they need and acquire that information, and whether MSRB is in a position to acquire such information in a reliable manner for posting to the system. They said that the planning will focus on how data are organized in the system and the parameters by which different types of users might want to search the data. MSRB staff also said that as the market in general has increasingly come to rely on the EMMA website, they will consider the needs of institutional investors and issuers as well as individual investors. MSRB staff told us that once the board approves the 5-year plan, they will release a summary version of it to the public.

Transparency Program Expenses Increased Significantly from Fiscal Years 2004 through 2010

As table 9 shows, MSRB's expenses related to developing and operating its Transparency Programs increased significantly over recent years, from about $4.8 million in fiscal year 2004 to about $11.3 million in fiscal year 2010, or from 35 percent to 49 percent of MSRB's total expenses. Table 9 also shows MSRB's total expenses increasing over 70 percent between fiscal year 2004 and fiscal year 2010, from about $13.6 million to about $23.1 million.

MSRB stated that its total operating expenses increased to approximately $26.1 million in fiscal year 2011 (a 13 percent increase over those of fiscal year 2010), and that it anticipates that its total operating expenses will increase to approximately $29.4 million in fiscal year 2012 (a 27 percent increase over those of fiscal year 2010).

Table 9. MSRB Expenses, Fiscal Years 2004-2010

Year ended September 30

Expenses	2004	2005	2006	2007	2008	2009	2010
Market Information Transparency Programs and operationsa	$4,769,029	$7,216,980	$7,240,392	$6,844,783	$7,224,140	$10,073,932	$11,319,323
Administration and operations	3,754,430	4,514,109	4,619,281	5,648,682	4,619,132	5,612,560	5,909,092
Rulemaking and policy development	2,930,805	3,613,446	3,605,787	3,614,750	4,253,688	2,994,537	3,030,192
Board and committee	1,110,212	1,134,080	1,283,029	1,566,723	1,545,968	1,473,049	1,625,522
Professional qualifications	744,469	731,878	736,268	758,473	741,022	616,748	463,133
Education and communications	321,444	212,660	149,601	178,870	177,601	510,434	784,146
Total expenses	$13,630,389	$17,423,153	$17,634,358	$18,612,281	$18,561,551	$ 21,281,260	$23,131,408

Source: GAO analysis of MSRB audited financial statements.

aIn fiscal year 2004, MSRB operated MSIL, which collected, stored, and provided access to certain municipal securities market information. The data in this system were only available to subscribers. In fiscal year 2005, MSRB implemented the Real-Time Trade Reporting System, but again the data in the system were only available to subscribers. During fiscal years 2008 and 2009, MSRB implemented the EMMA website, which replaced MSIL and offered market disclosures and data, including RTRS data, to the public.

Table 10. MSRB Revenues, Fiscal Years 2004-2010

Year ended September 30

Revenues	2004	2005	2006	2007	2008	2009	2010
Underwriting assessment fees	$9,752,383	$11,149,597	$9,852,226	$12,456,134	$12,188,220	$10,837,652	$13,984,780
Transaction fees	5,421,603	5,611,792	6,198,630	6,893, 813	7,723,365	7,150,905	6,940,551
Annual fees	744,800	712,300	684,800	663,300	644,864	622,700	1,010,321
Data subscriber fees	238,523	466,000	406,295	375,066	390,210	441,392	509,547
Professional qualification examination fees[a]	N/A[b]	N/A	N/A	N/A	N/A	N/A	92,220
Initial fees	12,900	8,800	9,600	8,500	8,800	8,400	8,500
Investment return	107,802	210,043	601,322	1,008,422	1,123,096	533,667	92,715
Publications and other Income	258,347	22,909	16,067	69,859	72,194	33,268	41,612
Total revenues	$16,536,358	$18,181,441	$17,768,940	$21,475,094	$22,150,749	$19,627,984	$22,680,246
Underwriting assessment and transaction fees as a percentage of total revenue	92%	92%	90%	90%	90%	92%	92%

Source: GAO analysis of MSRB audited financial statements.

[a]In November 2009, MSRB filed a new rule that established an examination fee of $60 assessed on persons taking certain qualification examinations as of January 4, 2010. These examinations include the Series 51 (Municipal Fund Securities Limited Principal Qualification Examination), Series 52 (Municipal Securities Representative Qualification Examination), and Series 53 (Municipal Securities Principal Qualification Examination).

[b]Not applicable.

MSRB stated that a significant part of these increases are due to anticipated expenses related to the Transparency Programs, such as replacing aging and outdated technology systems and new technology initiatives. Other anticipated expenses are related to rulemaking activities required under the Dodd-Frank Wall Street Reform and Consumer Protection Act (Dodd-Frank Act) and other information systems needed to fulfill MSRB's mission.

MSRB has relied mostly on the underwriting and transaction fees it collects from broker-dealers to fund its expenses, including those related to the Transparency Programs.

Table 10 shows that these fees accounted for between 90 and 92 percent of total revenues for fiscal years 2004-2010.

Table 10 also shows that MSRB's total revenues declined by 11.4 percent from fiscal year 2008 to fiscal year 2009, which MSRB attributed to the economic crisis and consequent decrease in transaction fees and underwriting assessment fees collected.

This decline in revenues occurred when expenses were increasing, as shown in figure 2.

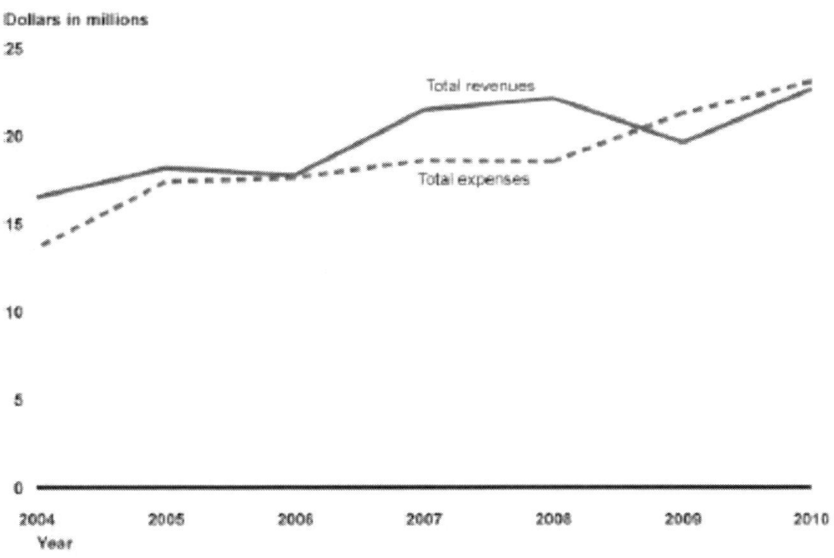

Source: MSRB audited financial statements.

Figure 2. MSRB Revenues and Expenses, Fiscal Years 2004 through 2010.

MSRB Increased the Transaction Fee and Levied a New Technology Fee to Generate Additional Revenues

To establish a more stable long-term revenue base as well as ensure a more equitable allocation of assessments among the municipal broker-dealers that fund MSRB's operations, MSRB authorized changes to its revenue sources in fiscal year 2011 that it expects will generate significant new revenues. First, MSRB increased the transaction fee charged to broker-dealers from $0.005 per $1,000 par value to $0.01 per $1,000 par value on most municipal securities sales transactions reported to MSRB. The new fee became effective in January 2011. MSRB expects the increased transaction fee to generate an estimated $7 million annually. Second, effective January 2011, dealers in municipal securities are required to pay a technology fee of $1.00 per transaction for all sales transactions. MSRB expects the technology fee to generate an estimated $8.5 million annually. MSRB stated that the technology fee would be transitional in nature and that it would review the fee periodically to determine whether it should continue to be assessed.[4]

MSRB said that these new and increased fees are necessary because its expenses have increased significantly as a consequence of its capital investments in technology and the regulatory responsibilities it has assumed under the Dodd-Frank Act. MSRB said it would use the new technology fee to establish a technology renewal fund, which would be segregated for accounting purposes. The technology renewal fund is intended to fund replacement of aging and outdated technology and to fund new technology initiatives. For example, MSRB noted that certain of the existing public information systems it operates, including RTRS, now rely on dated technology and can be expected to need comprehensive reengineering in the coming years. In addition, MSRB said that it will need to develop information systems to facilitate its increased regulatory responsibilities under the Dodd-Frank Act, which, among other things, broadened its mission to include the protection of municipal issuers and extended its regulatory authority to include municipal advisers.

The Dodd-Frank Act provided for additional revenue sources for MSRB, although these revenues are unlikely to represent a significant source of funding. The Dodd-Frank Act expanded the regulatory jurisdiction of MSRB to include municipal advisers. MSRB amended its rules in November 2010 to begin collecting initial fees ($100) and annual registration fees ($500) for municipal advisers. However, MSRB officials said that they did not anticipate these fees would provide a revenue stream comparable to what MSRB receives from all fees on broker-dealer activities, including the transaction, underwriting, and technology fees previously discussed. The Dodd-Frank Act also mandated that SEC and the Financial Industry Regulatory Authority, Inc., remit to MSRB a portion of the fines collected for violation of MSRB rules. Effective October 2010, SEC must remit half of the fines it collects to MSRB, and FINRA must remit one-third, although that amount may be modified by agreement among SEC, MSRB, and FINRA. MSRB stated that the amounts actually received will be dependent on the level of enforcement by SEC and MSRB and is expected to vary considerably from year to year.

APPENDIX V. SELECTED SEC CASES AND OPINIONS INVOLVING EXCESSIVE MUNICIPAL SECURITIES MARKUPS AND MARKDOWNS

Since the early 1970s, several Securities and Exchange Commission cases and opinions have addressed instances in which broker-dealers charged excessive markups or markdowns in municipal securities transactions with customers. Table 11 summarizes the details of a few of these cases.

Table 11. Selected SEC Cases and Opinions Involving Excessive Municipal Securities Markups and Markdowns, 1970-2011

Case	Year	Findings
SEC v. Charles A. Morris & Associates, Inc., et al (U.S. District Court)	1974	SEC ordered a permanent injunction against the firm. Among other things, the District Court and SEC found the defendant had been selling bonds at prices not reasonably related to the prevailing market prices and charging markups ranging from 25 percent to 100 percent over the prices at which recent interdealer trades occurred.
Staten Securities Corporation (SEC Review of NASD Disciplinary Proceedings)a	1982	SEC upheld NASD's findings that the firm's markups, ranging from 5.1 percent to 6.7 percent, were excessive. SEC found that the securities were readily available in the marketplace with easily ascertainable prices, the firm was not atrisk with respect to any of the transactions, and the firm did not incur any unusual expense in effecting the transactions. SEC also stated in this case that markups of 5 percent or less are not necessarily fair and reasonable. SEC upheld NASD's penalties, which censured the firm, imposed joint and individual fines of $2,000, and prohibited

Table 11. (Continued)

Case	Year	Findings
		the firm's president and principal shareholder from supervising or effecting principal transactions in municipal securities with public customers until he took and passed a municipal securities principal qualification examination.
First Honolulu Securities, Inc. (SEC Review of NASD Disciplinary Proceedings)	1993	SEC upheld NASD's findings of violation for markups above 5 percent, but it setaside NASD's findings of violations for markups below 5 percent. SEC noted in its decision that, while it agreed that the markups below 5 percent were likely unfair, it may not have been clear when the transactions occurred in 1990 that markups between 4 percent and 5 percent usually are unfair, since SEC had not dealt with enforcement cases for markups below 5 percent until 1993. SEC also noted that it set aside findings of excessive markups that were below 4 percent because NASD had not introduced any evidence to establish the unfairness of markups at those levels, but noted that markups below 4 percent may well have been unfair. The firm was censured and fined $7,400.
Mark David Anderson (SEC Opinion)	2003	SEC imposed substantial monetary sanctions and a cease and desist order against a broker-dealer who, in the mid-1990s, had charged retail customers markups ranging from 1.42 percent to 5 percent and markdowns ranging from 3.02 percent to 5.64 percent. Most of the transactions in question were executed on a "riskless principal" basis, in which the defendant knew he had a buyer and a seller in place prior to executing the trade. SEC concluded that the markups and markdowns deviated significantly from industry norms. SEC rejected the defendant's argument that his aggregate prices were fair because the securities offered competitive yields.

Sources: Lexis, SEC, and Westlaw.

[a]The National Association of Securities Dealers (NASD) formerly acted as the self-regulatory organization for broker-dealers. In July 2007, NASD assumed the broker-dealer regulatory functions of the New York Stock Exchange and became FINRA.

APPENDIX VI: REGULATORS' POLICIES AND PROCEDURES FOR MONITORING COMPLIANCE WITH MSRB RULES G-30 AND G-14

The Financial Industry Regulatory Authority, Inc., the federal banking regulators, and the Securities and Exchange Commission use a variety of methods to help ensure broker-dealers' compliance with rules issued by the

Municipal Securities Rulemaking Board. We reviewed their written policies and procedures to understand how they assess broker-dealers' compliance with MSRB Rules G-30 (fair and reasonable pricing) and G14 (timely, accurate, and complete trade reporting). FINRA has established electronic surveillances of data reported to MSRB's Real-Time Transaction Reporting System, by which it analyzes the data to generate "alerts" for potential violations of certain MSRB rules. FINRA, in certain circumstances, refers potential violations by bank dealers to the appropriate federal banking regulators for further investigation. During the period of our review, MSRB Rule G-16 required FINRA and the federal banking regulators to conduct routine examinations of the firms under their jurisdiction once every 2 years for compliance with all MSRB rules and other applicable laws.[1] The SEC's Office of Compliance Inspections and Examinations also conducts oversight activities through examinations of selected broker-dealers.

FINRA

Rule G-30

FINRA utilizes parameters to help target its surveillance for fair pricing and markup violations. For example, a surveillance program established to identify transactions that were not executed at the prevailing market price would flag any transactions priced outside of a certain range of comparable prices. Similarly, a surveillance program established to identify excessive markups or markdowns would flag any transactions with markups or markdowns above a specified percentage of the contemporaneous costs (for markups) or proceeds (for markdowns). FINRA staff stated that these parameters are merely guidelines to assist them in identifying transactions for further review. FINRA analysts follow a series of steps to determine whether alerts generated by the surveillances represent actual violations of Rule G-30. Specifically:

- The analyst uses various data sources, such as Bloomberg, MSRB's Electronic Municipal Market Access website, or audit trail data, to verify the information in the alert and confirm or establish the prevailing market price for the municipal security at the time of the trade in question.

- If necessary, the analyst asks the firm for documentation and an explanation of how it determined that its price and markup or markdown were fair and reasonable.
- After reviewing the firm's documentation, the analyst prepares a memorandum recommending a particular disposition for review and approval by FINRA managers.

In their G-30 compliance reviews during broker-dealer examinations, FINRA examiners check for price manipulation and excessive markups and markdowns. The manipulation module of FINRA's examination tool kit includes several questions and warning signs that help examiners identify whether broker-dealer firms intentionally tried to manipulate prices. FINRA's examination tool kit also contains a module to help examiners identify excessive markups or markdowns. Examiners follow a series of steps:

- Examiners collect a variety of records from the firm, such as order tickets and confirmations for a given sample of transactions, as well as daily transaction reports.
- Using MSRB data, they identify a comparison transaction that best represents the market (i.e., the prevailing market price) for each sample security at the time of each sample customer transaction.
- Using the comparison transaction data and records collected from the firm, examiners calculate the markups and markdowns that the firm charged on the sample transactions.

For markups or markdowns outside of specific parameters, examiners request an explanation from the firm. Again, the parameters are merely guidelines to assist them in identifying transactions for further review.

- Examiners consider the facts and circumstances of each individual case and, when necessary, consult with FINRA fixed-income experts to substantiate violations.

Rule G-14

FINRA's periodic late trade reporting surveillance identifies transactions reported more than 15 minutes after they occurred, with analysts following a similar review process as they follow for pricing and markup or markdown alerts.[2]

- FINRA reviews MSRB transaction data and selects firms with higher levels of potential noncompliance during a given surveillance period.
- As with surveillances for pricing and markups, analysts use various data sources, such as Bloomberg, the EMMA website, or audit trail information to provide context for each case.
- If necessary, the analyst asks the firm for documentation, including an explanation for the late reporting and any trade memorandums in support of that explanation, a copy of the firm's written supervisory procedures regarding municipal securities transaction reporting, and any evidence of the firm's own review of the transactions in question.
- The analyst reviews the documentation and prepares a memorandum recommending a particular disposition for review and approval by FINRA managers.

In their G-14 compliance reviews conducted during examinations, using a sample of trades from the firm's trading blotters, FINRA examiners conduct a "failure to report" review to detect transactions that the firm effected but failed to report to MSRB. They also check whether firms have filed and kept current a Form RTRS with MSRB. This form contains information that ensures that the firm's trade reports can be processed correctly. Finally, examiners look for unreported and inaccurately reported trades, as well as late reported trades that would not have been detected by FINRA's surveillance activities. In doing so, they adhere to the following procedures:

- Examiners review monthly RTRS statistics on trades that the firm executed or cleared during the review period. They select a time period for review and run statistical reports related to each broker-dealer firm's trade reporting for that time period. They also obtain detailed trade information from MSRB.
- Examiners then select a sample of trades from the time period they chose for review.
- For the selected sample, they request and review order tickets and confirmations from the firm and compare the RTRS information to the information on those documents, making note of differences between the two sources. For discrepancies noted, they attempt to determine the root cause of the apparent violations and, if necessary, expand their sample to confirm the violation.

Federal Banking Regulators

Rule G-30

The Office of the Comptroller of the Currency, the Federal Deposit Insurance Corporation, and the Board of Governors of the Federal Reserve System constitute the federal banking regulators that oversee those banks that are registered as dealers of municipal securities. In general, the three federal banking regulators' examination policies and procedures require bank examiners to select a sample of the bank dealer's transactions, review the relevant bank documentation and MSRB data for those transactions, and analyze the data to evaluate whether any prices appear to be unfair or unreasonable.

Rule G-14

Federal banking regulator officials told us that bank examiners obtain and review MSRB transaction data prior to their on-site examinations. When conducting on-site bank dealer examinations, federal banking examiners generally select a sample of the bank dealers' transactions for a given review period. They typically request and review copies of the bank's transaction records for the review period and compare the bank's records with MSRB transaction data to ensure that the bank reported all of its trades to MSRB accurately and on time.

OCIE

Rule G-30

In checking for G-30 compliance during broker-dealer examinations, OCIE examiners generally take some or all of the following steps:

- Examiners review MSRB data to select a sample of the firm's transactions that appear to have higher markups than other reported transactions in a given review period.
- Using order tickets, confirmations, and information on contemporaneous costs or proceeds, they calculate the markups or markdowns the firm charged on the sample transactions.
- Examiners ask the firm to explain cases that fall outside of certain parameters.

Rule G-14

In checking for G-14 compliance during broker-dealer examinations, OCIE examiners generally do the following:

- Examiners select a population of municipal transactions for a given review period.
- They compare the MSRB trade information with the information on the firm's purchase and sales blotter to determine whether all transactions were reported.
- They also select a sample of order tickets and confirmations for the trades and compare that information with the MSRB report to check for accuracy of reporting.

End Notes

[1] Federal Reserve Flow of Funds Accounts of the United States, December 8, 2011. This figure comprises securities held directly by individual investors (51 percent) or through investment management companies such as mutual funds, money market mutual funds, closed-end funds, and exchange-traded funds (24 percent). Insurance companies and commercial banks hold most of the remaining securities

[2] Liquidity refers to the relative ability of a security to be readily convertible into cash without substantial transaction costs or reduction of value. Price transparency refers to the degree to which information regarding quotations for securities (pretrade transparency) and the prices and volume of transactions (post-trade transparency) is made publicly available in the securities market.

[3] SROs are exchanges and associations that operate and govern the markets, and that are subject to oversight by the Securities and Exchange Commission.

[4] Section 977 of the Dodd-Frank Act contains a provision that requires MSRB, FINRA, and SEC to meet at least twice a year to discuss their respective work in the regulation of municipal securities trading and to share information about their respective rules and examination and enforcement activities related to municipal securities. Pub. L. No.111- 203, § 975(b)(5), 124 Stat. 1376, 1920 (2010).

[5] Dodd-Frank Wall Street Reform and Consumer Protection Act, Pub. L. No. 111-203, §977, 124 Stat. 1376, 1924 (2010).

[6] A broker's broker is a broker-dealer that executes securities transactions exclusively with other broker-dealers.

[7] The fixed-income inspections we reviewed were of the National Association of Securities Dealers (NASD), which formerly acted as the SRO for broker-dealers. In July 2007, NASD assumed the broker-dealer regulatory functions of the New York Stock Exchange and became FINRA.

[8] An underwriter is a broker-dealer that purchases a new issue of municipal securities for resale in a primary offering. Often a group of underwriters, known as an underwriting syndicate, forms to purchase new issues. The underwriting spread is the difference between the

amount underwriters pay an issuer for its securities and the amount they receive from selling the securities in the primary offering.

[9] Institutional investors participate in the primary market by buying large blocks of municipal securities directly from the underwriters. Individual investors may be able to participate in the primary market, particularly—but not exclusively—if the issuer establishes a retail order period. During a retail order period, underwriters or the underwriting syndicate seeks orders only from retail customers. Issuers determine whether a primary offering will have a retail order period, the length of the retail order period, and who qualifies as a retail customer. Underwriters told us that some issuers defined retail customers as individuals but might also include entities that represent individuals, such as trusts.

[10] Although MSRB trade data do not distinguish between individual and institutional investors, most broker-dealers we spoke with said that their individual investor clients trade in amounts of $100,000 or less. Our analysis of MSRB trade data showed that in 2010 about 82 percent of dealer sales to investors of newly issued fixed-rate bonds were for $100,000 or less and that about 97 percent of all such trades were for $1 million or less. However, individual investors can make larger trades; for example, one broker-dealer we interviewed said some of the firm's individual customers buy $250,000 to $1 million blocks of municipal securities.

[11] For interest on a municipal security to qualify as exempt from the investor's gross income for federal income tax purposes, the issuer must meet a number of requirements in the federal income tax code and regulations. Some taxable municipal securities were issued in 2009 and 2010 under the Build America Bonds program adopted as part of the American Recovery and Reinvestment Act of 2009. An issuer may also issue taxable securities if the purpose of the issuer's financing does not meet certain public purpose or public use tests under the federal tax rules, such as in the case of private activity bonds.

[12] As of October 3, 2011, Bloomberg tracked over 46,000 municipal issuers and obligors as well as 1,138,405 outstanding unique municipal securities, as identified by their Committee on Uniform Security Identification Procedures (CUSIP) numbers. Generally, a CUSIP number uniquely identifies municipal securities in each maturity for a given primary market issuance.

[13] We obtained data on the number of companies listed on the New York Stock Exchange, the NASDAQ Stock Market, and the NYSE Amex as of December 31, 2010, from the 2010 annual reports of NYSE Euronext and NASDAQ QMX.

[14] For example, municipal bonds can have a "put," or "tender," feature, giving the investor the right to surrender the securities to the issuer at specified dates and at a predetermined price (usually par), or a "call" feature that gives issuers the right to call, or redeem, a security prior to the stated date of maturity.

[15] We derived this statistic by dividing 15,051 (the average daily number of unique municipal securities traded in 2010, according to MSRB) by 1,138,405 (the number of outstanding municipal securities as of October 3, 2011, according to Bloomberg).

[16] According to MSRB, the top 10 underwriting firms underwrote over 70 percent of primary market issuance volume (by par amount) in 2010 and in 2011. Additionally, the top 10 broker-dealer firms executed about 55 percent of secondary market trades in 2010 and 2011, and the top 200 broker-dealer firms accounted for 98 percent of all municipal trade volume (by par amount) in 2010 and 2011. The remaining approximately 1,600 firms were less active in the municipal securities market as they were not primarily engaged in municipal securities underwriting, research, or trading.

[17] Most broker-dealers execute trades as the principal by trading securities from their proprietary accounts.

[18] Broker's brokers execute transactions primarily with broker-dealers for a fee and do not maintain proprietary inventories of securities. Municipal broker's brokers are registered as such through MSRB. Other over-the-counter fixed-income markets also use interdealer brokers to facilitate transactions in the secondary market.

[19] In a broker's broker bid wanted, the broker's broker typically disseminates information about the securities for sale electronically and then contacts various broker-dealers by phone to solicit bids (institutional Investors and broker-dealers can also customize their own bids wanted through Bloomberg). Besides arranging bids wanted, broker's brokers told us that they might facilitate situation trading, which is generally used for institutional-sized trades. In situation trading, broker's brokers find buyers for a broker-dealer's securities at a prespecified price set by the broker-dealer.

[20] The electronic trading platforms that broker-dealers told us they regularly used were registered with SEC as ATSs under Regulation ATS. The regulation defines an ATS as an organization, association, person, group of persons, or system that provides a marketplace or facility that brings together buyers and sellers of securities or otherwise performs the functions commonly performed by a stock exchange. However, the ATS does not set rules governing the conduct of the subscribers other than its ATS trading activities, nor does it discipline subscribers other than by excluding them from trading.

[21] MSRB also writes rules regulating municipal advisers that provide advice to or on behalf of municipal entities or obligated persons with respect to municipal financial products, the issuance of municipal securities, and certain solicitations of municipal entities and obligated persons. Nearly 200 registered broker-dealers, as well as over 500 other firms, are registered with MSRB as municipal advisers.

[22] On December 16, 2011, SEC approved a MSRB proposed rule change that included an amendment to MSRB Rule G-16, which had required FINRA and the federal banking regulators to examine broker-dealers at least once every 2 calendar years to determine their compliance with all applicable MSRB rules, as well as other SEC rules and regulations. The amended rule allows for up to a 4-year examination cycle for FINRA member firms, consistent with FINRA's existing requirement for examinations cycles for all other FINRA members. According to MSRB, broker-dealer firms that present higher risks would be likely examined on an annual basis, while other firms would be examined every 2 to 4 years, depending on the risks they presented. Cycle examination frequencies for FINRA member broker-dealer firms would be reassessed at least on an annual basis.

[23] In contrast, in the equities market, tradable quotes are readily available for all securities listed on the exchanges. Under SEC rules, broker-dealers that sell equity securities to individual or institutional investors must guarantee the National Best Bid and Offer (NBBO)—the best available ask price when the security is purchased and the best available bid price when it is sold. The NBBO is updated throughout the day to show the highest bid and lowest offers for all equity securities on all exchanges and market makers and is publicly available. In the municipal securities market, pricing evaluation services provide daily estimates for most outstanding securities to subscribers. However, participants said that they used these estimates primarily to assign values to municipal securities portfolios and did not generally consider them executable trade prices in the face of alternative sources of reliable and timely information.

[24] MSRB Rule G-30 requires that broker-dealers charge investors fair and reasonable aggregate prices. For most municipal securities trades, these prices reflect the market value of the

security, trading costs, and the compensation that the broker-dealer receives on the transaction.

[25] MSRB has been taking steps over a number of years to improve post-trade price transparency in the municipal securities markets. Prior to 1995, there was no systematic and comprehensive dissemination of either post-trade or pretrade information for municipal securities. In 1995, MSRB began next-day public dissemination of certain trades between broker-dealers. By 2003, MSRB was collecting and disseminating price data on all municipal securities transactions the morning after the trade date, but this information was not available to the general public. Real-time trade reporting began in 2005 with the implementation of RTRS and public dissemination of these data in 2008.

[26] Market participants and regulators explained they used these trades because trades between broker-dealers do not include compensation, which broker-dealers include in the aggregate price of a security when they trade with investors.

[27] A yield curve is a graph plotting the yields for securities of the same quality with maturities ranging from the shortest to the longest available. One commonly used benchmark yield curve plots yields for highly rated state general obligation securities. The curve allows users to compare bonds with different maturities and characteristics. For example, if three different securities offer yields below, at, and above the appropriate benchmark yields, respectively, the broker-dealer can use her judgment to decide whether or not these differences are warranted.

[28] There are no direct federal requirements on municipal issuers to produce or disseminate specific items of disclosure to the marketplace. Instead, the municipal securities disclosure regime is based on a combination of indirect disclosure obligations established through broker-dealers' role as underwriters in primary market issuances and voluntary issuer disclosures. Market participants have expressed frustration regarding the resulting lack of uniformity in the completeness and timeliness of issuer disclosures available in the municipal market, particularly in the secondary market. Section 976 of the Dodd-Frank Act also requires us to report on issues related to disclosure requirements for municipal issuers by July 2012, and this work is ongoing.

[29] Bond insurance provides securities with the rating of the bond insurer and guarantees investors timely interest payments and, if the issuers default, the return of principal. Market participants we spoke with agreed that the widespread use of bond insurance prior to the recent financial crisis significantly simplified the process of determining trade prices. The homogenization of the credit quality of most municipal securities allowed market participants to rely primarily on the creditworthiness of these few monoline insurers instead of assessing the credit quality of the underlying securities. However, during the recent financial crisis, many of these insurers suffered financial losses brought on by their exposure to troubled mortgage-backed securities and were subsequently downgraded. According to Thomson Reuters data in the 2006 and 2011 Bond Buyer Yearbook, in 2005, nine highly rated bond insurers insured about 57.1 percent of new issue volume (or 51 percent of newly issued securities). By 2010, there was only one active bond insurer in the market, providing insurance to approximately 6.2 percent of new issue volume (or 12 percent of newly issued securities).

[30] Interest rates increases tend to lower a security's value because its discounted cash flows (that is, the value of future expected cash receipts at a common date) fall as interest rates increase.

[31] MSRB trade prices reflect the aggregate prices that broker-dealers charged or paid when selling or buying securities, respectively. For trades with investors, these aggregate prices

include the compensation that broker-dealers charged or paid investors when selling securities to or buying securities from them, respectively.

[32] For more information on our methodology for this analysis, see appendix II. For regression analysis results supporting our findings for all years of analysis (2005-2010), see appendix III.

[33] For each trade, the relative price is the price of the broker-dealer sale or purchase to an investor as a percentage of the reoffering price (the price at which newly issued securities are sold to the public by the underwriter). The results of our analysis of broker-dealer sales to investors were statistically significant at the 1 percent level for all years. The results of our analysis of dealer purchases from customers were statistically significant at the 1 percent level for all years except 2009. For 2009, the relationship between relative trade price and trade amount was negative for dealer purchases from customers but was not statistically significantly different from zero.

[34] The results were the same for three different measures of spreads—the mean, outside, and inside spreads. The mean spread is the difference between the mean price on dealer sales and the mean price on dealer purchases to investors as a percentage of the mean price on dealer purchases. The outside spread is the difference between the highest price on dealer sales and the lowest price on dealer purchases to investors as a percentage of the lowest price on dealer purchases. Last, the inside spread is the difference between the lowest price on dealer sales and the highest price on a dealer purchases as a percentage of the highest price on dealer purchases. Mean, inside, and outside spreads were calculated for each security, for each trade size category (trade size was grouped into $10,000 increments). Our results were statistically significant at the 1 percent level for all three measures of spread for all years.

[35] See Richard C. Green, Burton Hollifield, and Norman Schürhoff, "Financial Intermediation and the Costs of Trading in an Opaque Market," Review of Financial Studies 20(2), March 2007, 275-314; Lawrence E. Harris and Michael S. Piwowar, "Secondary Trading Costs in the Municipal Bond Market," Journal of Finance 61(3), June 2006, 1361-97; and Securities and Exchange Commission, Offices of Economic Analysis and Municipal Securities, Report on Transactions in Municipal Securities, Washington D.C., July 1, 2004. Available at www.sec.gov/news/ studies/ munireport2004.pdf.

[36] See Richard C. Green, Burton Hollifield, and Norman Schürhoff, "Dealer Intermediation and Price Behavior in the Aftermarket for New Bond Issues," Journal of Financial Economics 86 (2007), 643-82; and Securities and Exchange Commission, Report on Transactions in Municipal Securities.

[37] See Harris and Piwowar, "Secondary Trading Costs in the Municipal Bond Market."

[38] See Green, Hollifield, and Schürhoff, "Dealer Intermediation and Price Behavior." Other studies have noted potential evidence of broker-dealers' ability to use their position in the market to the detriment of investors. For example, one study suggests that broker-dealers exercise their market power by either disregarding crucial disclosure information or withholding it from buyers in order to sell securities at higher prices. (See Peter Schmitt, The Consequences of Poor Disclosure Enforcement in the Municipal Securities Market, DPC Data 2009). Another study suggests that when selling securities, broker-dealers opportunistically delay responses to price drops while immediately recognizing price increases. (See Richard C. Green, Dan Li, and Norman Schurhoff, "Price Discovery in Illiquid Markets: Do Financial Asset Prices Rise Faster Than They Fall?" Journal of Finance, Vol. 65 (5), October 2010).

[39] See Paul Shultz, The Market for New Issues of Municipal Bonds: The Roles of Transparency and Limited Access to Retail Investors, University of Notre Dame, January 2012.

[40] Institutional investors we spoke with said that it was their standard practice to maintain and trade only through internally approved broker-dealers that were continually reviewed for performance and conduct. A couple of investors noted that while they had relationships with many broker-dealers, they did the bulk of their trades through about 13 to19 percent of them.

[41] For example, of the nine individual investors we spoke with who traded municipal securities directly through broker-dealers, four had accounts with one broker, while the remaining five used two to four brokers to trade municipal securities (we also interviewed two individuals who invested in municipal securities through mutual funds).

[42] Market participants told us that retail broker-dealers were unlikely to have the same securities in inventory because of the variety of municipal securities available and the geographic fragmentation of the market, among other things.

[43] A broker-dealer that combines offerings with an electronic trading platform may also be able to expand by selling securities through other broker-dealer subscribers that may sell them to their clients.

[44] Full-service brokers provide personalized service to their investors, including research and investment advice.

[45] Through Bloomberg, institutional investors can customize their own bids wanted by sending out the details of the auction to Bloomberg users of their choice and receiving bids. Some institutional investors noted they usually solicited bids from their network of broker-dealers, which in turn solicited bids from their own customers. On the other hand, institutional investors are not involved in the broker's brokers' bids wanted. If a broker-dealer seeks the services of a broker's broker to sell an institutional investor's securities, the investor receives the anonymous highest bids and can decide to hold or sell the securities.

[46] Some broker's brokers offer anonymity by buying the securities from the selling dealer and then immediately selling them to another dealer that they lined up prior to executing the trade. For example, an institutional investor selling a large block of securities may ask a broker's broker to facilitate the trades and sell the securities in smaller blocks so as to maintain a stable price and not reveal the investor's trading strategy. For other transactions that do not require anonymity, broker's brokers reveal the names of both parties at the point of sale.

[47] According to Bloomberg staff, a subscription to Bloomberg services costs about $20,000 a year.

[48] See appendix IV for a discussion of MSRB's ongoing assessment of the EMMA website and related transparency programs and funding of these programs.

[49] These models create benchmark yield curves that allow investors to deem a price "cheap," "fair," or "rich" if it is below, at, or above the model's estimated market value.

[50] Certain disclosure, suitability, and fair pricing obligations of a broker-dealer under MSRB rules may be deemed fulfilled in connection with a transaction between the broker-dealer and an investor that constitutes a Sophisticated Municipal Market Professional (SMMP) with respect to such transaction. MSRB recently proposed changes to its definition of SMMP to include individuals with at least $50 million invested in municipal assets who believed and affirmatively attested to their broker-dealers that they could independently evaluate investment risks and market value both in general and for specific transactions. The previous definition excluded individual investors and included institutional investors with at least $100 million invested in municipal securities. The proposal noted that these

changes were the result of investors' increased access to electronic trading platforms and issuer disclosure information, among others things, as well as the movement to align MSRB rules with FINRA rules. See MSRB 2011-63, November 8, 2011.

[51] As mentioned earlier, while MSRB's EMMA website provides a central repository of issuer disclosure information, MSRB does not have the authority to regulate the content or timing of these disclosures. For more information on investors' concerns with issuer disclosures, see the transcript to SEC's Hearing on the Municipal Securities market, December 2010, available at http://www.sec.gov/spotlight/ municipal securities.shtml.

[52] SEC held three hearings on the municipal securities market, including one in San Francisco, CA; one in Washington, DC; and one in Birmingham, AL. SEC staff told us that SEC originally planned to hold more hearings but were unable to because of budget constraints. Instead, staff said that they held a number of "mini muni" hearings, meeting with a variety of municipal securities market stakeholders at SEC's offices.

[53] Commissioner Elisse B. Walter, U.S. Securities and Exchange Commission, Key Note Address at the National Association of Bond Lawyers (NABL) 35th Bond Attorneys' Workshop. San Antonio, TX, October 28, 2010.

[54] A limit order is an order to buy or sell a security at a specified price.

[55] Academic researchers point out that both municipal and corporate securities were predominantly traded on the New York Stock Exchange until the 1920s and the 1940s, respectively. They argue that the switch from an exchange to an over-the-counter trading venue was most likely the result of the concurrent increase in institutional investors' participation in the markets. See Bruno Biais and Richard C. Green, "The Microstructure of the Bond Market in the 20th Century," Institut d'Economie Industrielle Working Paper No. 482, August 29, 2007.

[56] Some banks designate a department or division to engage in municipal securities underwriting, trading, and sales; financial advisory or consultant services for issuers of municipal securities; or processing and clearance activities for municipal securities. These entities must register as municipal securities dealers with SEC and provide a copy of their registration to the appropriate federal banking regulator. As of December 2011, there were 11 bank dealers under OCC's jurisdiction, 8 under FDIC's, and 11 under the Federal Reserve's. However, an OCC staff member told us that the number of municipal securities dealers under each banking regulator's jurisdiction could fluctuate as banks registered and withdrew as municipal securities dealers or switched charters among the three banking regulators.

[57] A settlement failure occurs when delivery or receipt of securities does not take place on the settlement date for a transaction between two broker-dealers.

[58] MSRB Rule G-18 addresses a broker-dealer's responsibility to make a reasonable effort to obtain a fair and reasonable price for customers in agency transactions (those in which the broker-dealer buys or sells securities on behalf of and under the instruction of another party—typically the customer—but does not take any securities into his own account). However, Rule G-18 does not address the broker-dealer's compensation for agency transactions, which are in the form of commissions rather than markups or markdowns. Rule G-30(b) addresses commissions, which differ from markups and markdowns in that they are typically set fees per security or transaction rather than fees based on the security's prevailing market price. A broker-dealer acting in an agency capacity must disclose the commission charged to customers as a separate item on the transaction confirmation.

[59] For a discussion of numeric guidelines related to Rule G-30, see the MSRB Rule Book 2011, 239 (Report on Pricing, September 26, 1980). Available at http://www.msrb. org/msrb1/

pdfs/MSRBRulebook.pdf. By comparison, guidance issued in connection with FINRA's rule on fair commissions and markups (IM-2440-1) includes a statement that markups and markdowns on securities transactions, which include debt securities transactions (bond transactions), generally should not exceed 5 percent. However, this guidance is not definitive and, if factored into a markup analysis appropriately, is only one of several items considered. IM-2440-1 also states that a higher percentage of the markup customarily applies to a common stock transaction than to a bond transaction of the same size.

[60] There are three ways for broker-dealers to report their trades to the RTRS. First, NSCC operates an RTRS portal that may be used for any trade record submission or trade modification. Second, broker-dealers can report customer transactions (but not most interdealer transactions) to MSRB's web-based RTRS portal. Third, broker-dealers must report most interdealer transactions through NSCC's Real-Time Trade Matching (RTTM) portal, which feeds into the RTRS.

[61] Rule G-14 provides exemptions to this 15-minute window. For example, dealers have until the end of the RTRS business day to report trades in certain short-term (less than 9 months in maturity) instruments, including variable- rate instruments, auction-rate products, and commercial paper. RTRS entries for customer trades require a variety of details, such as the CUSIP number, trade date and time, settlement date, par amount and dollar price of the trade, the yield (with limited exceptions), and the commission (if applicable), as well as whether it was a buy or a sell and a principal or agency transaction.

[62] The memorandum of understanding between MSRB and FINRA, created in 2006 and substantially broadened under a new memorandum of understanding entered into in September 2011, specifies multiple ways in which the two SROs have agreed to work together to ensure broker-dealer compliance with MSRB rules. For example, the memorandum specifies what kinds of information MSRB will share with FINRA; how MSRB will support FINRA's surveillance, examination, and enforcement activities, including providing technical support and referring potential rule violations to FINRA; and how often MSRB and FINRA will meet regarding specific regulatory activities.

[63] FINRA officials told us that the number of alerts does not necessarily equate to the number of cases they opened. For instance, FINRA might open a single case in response to hundreds of alerts for a broker-dealer firm.

[64] FINRA officials noted that in cases where broker-dealers that were FINRA members committed pricing violations that did not warrant further review because of the limited nature of the violations or mitigating factors, FINRA typically sought restitution on behalf of customers for any losses the customers incurred in violative transactions.

[65] Percentages total more than 100 percent because of rounding.

[66] Although the markups and markdowns in the examinations we reviewed ranged from about 2 percent to about 10 percent, FINRA officials noted that there is no upper limit on markup or markdown percentages that examiners would question.

[67] We obtained information from OCIE on broker-dealer examinations conducted from 2002 through 2010 and on the MSRB rule violations cited. However, the Super Tracking and Reporting System (STARS), the OCIE database that stores this information, does not allow users to conduct automatic searches for certain examination components, such as products reviewed. Therefore, the list of approximately 1,100 examinations and MSRB violations we received likely did not capture all of the examinations OCIE conducted with a municipal component from 2002 through 2010. OCIE is aware of the deficiency with the database, and staff stated that SEC is currently developing new systems with improved search capabilities. In addition, as noted above, OCIE does not consistently review for compliance with all

MSRB rules in every examination it conducts. For these reasons, we chose not to present statistics from the broker-dealer examination information we received from OCIE. However, we did review selected OCIE broker-dealer examinations to observe how OCIE examiners assessed them for compliance with certain MSRB rules, particularly G-30 and G-14.

[68] Unrated bonds would likely require the broker-dealer to do more research, which could increase the expense of executing the transaction. Similarly, low-rated bonds may be more challenging for broker-dealers to market to potential buyers than well-known, highly rated securities, possibly resulting in higher markups.

[69] FINRA's IM-2440-2 states that in a debt security transaction with a customer, a brokerdealer's markup or markdown must be calculated from the prevailing market price of that security. This price is typically the broker-dealer's cost or proceeds from a recent interdealer purchase or sale in the same CUSIP (contemporaneous cost or proceeds) to which the firm was a party. To avoid this pricing policy, the broker-dealer must show that, given particular circumstances, the contemporaneous cost or proceeds were not indicative of the prevailing market price. In the event that the broker-dealer does not have a recent interdealer transaction to identify the current prevailing market price of the bond, FINRA (in IM-2440-2) provides a hierarchy of alternatives for determining its prevailing market price.

[70] The proposed guidance provides several illustrations to explain how broker-dealers would determine the prevailing market price in different situations. However, according to MSRB officials, one of the illustrations conflicts with, and certain principles underlying the proposed guidance may not be entirely consistent with, Draft Rule G-43, a proposed rule addressing the use of broker's brokers that MSRB has twice issued for comment since February 2011. MSRB officials stated that they were waiting to finalize the guidance on pricing until they had considered all comments on Draft Rule G-43.

[71] Officials from the Depository Trust and Clearing Corporation (DTCC), the parent company of DTC and NSCC, stated that NSCC typically did not track settlement failures by type of security (for example, municipal, equity, and so on). However, NSCC analyzed municipal settlement failures in response to our request. DTCC officials also noted that DTC and NSCC did not clear and settle 100 percent of all trades, municipal or otherwise. However, they stated that DTC and NSCC likely handled the majority of municipal trades.

[72] OCIE's Market Oversight group examines SROs that are registered securities exchanges, FINRA (a national securities association), MSRB, the Public Company Accounting Oversight Board, and the Securities Investor Protection Corporation. OCIE's Clearing and Settlement group examines clearing agency SROs. In 2009, this group conducted inspections of DTC and NSCC, SROs that conduct clearance and settlement of municipal securities trades.

[73] OCIE transitioned several years ago to a risk-based approach to examining broker-dealers and investment advisors. OCIE staff stated that this approach permits the examination program to focus its resources on entities and issues that pose the highest risk for investors.

[74] OCIE's inspection findings are not public information.

[75] GAO-08-33.

[76] As noted earlier, we conducted a data reliability assessment of the MSRB trade data with respect to specific variables for our purpose, which was to understand how prices differ for institutional and individual investors. However, we did not assess the MSRB data's reliability for the transparency or regulatory purposes for which broker-dealers, investors, and regulators use the system.

[77] SEC Release No. 34-50699, November 18, 2004. The rule was part of a larger package of proposed rules and amendments related to fair administration and governance of SROs, which SEC has not finalized.

End Notes for Appendix I

[1] A derivative is a financial instrument created from or whose value depends upon the value of one or more separate assets or indexes of asset values.

[2] In an interest rate swap, the principal amount is not actually exchanged between the counterparties. The payments on an interest rate swap are a function of the (1) principal amount, (2) interest rates, and (3) the time elapsed between payments. The counterparties to the swap agree to exchange payments on specific dates, according to a predetermined formula.

[3] Beyond seeking cost savings, issuers may also use interest rate swaps to hedge interest rate risk in their debt portfolios, better manage their assets and liabilities, or gain access to different markets and their respective investor bases.

[4] Bond insurance guarantees investors timely interest payments and, if the issuers default, the return of principal. According to Thomson Reuters data in the 2006 and 2011 Bond Buyer Yearbook, in 2005, nine highly rated bond insurers insured about 57.1 percent of new issue volume (or 51 percent of newly issued securities). By 2010, there was only one active bond insurer in the market, providing insurance to approximately 6.2 percent of new issue volume (or 12 percent of newly issued securities). During the recent financial crisis, many of these insurers had suffered financial losses brought on by their exposure to troubled mortgage-backed securities and were subsequently downgraded.

[5] The Dodd-Frank Act provided the Securities and Exchange Commission (SEC) the authority to regulate security-based swaps, security-based swap dealers, and major security-based swap participants. SEC has proposed rules to implement this authority.

[6] The Dodd-Frank Act defines a swap dealer as any person that holds itself out as a dealer in swaps, makes a market in swaps, regularly enters into swaps with counterparties in the ordinary course of business for its own account, or engages in any activity causing the person to be commonly known as a dealer or market maker in swaps in connection with CFTC-regulated swaps. It defines a major swap participant as any person that is not a swap dealer and that meets any of the following criteria: maintains a substantial position in swaps, holds outstanding swaps that create substantial counterparty exposure, or is a highly leveraged financial entity. It defines special entities to include states and their political subdivisions (state agencies, cities, and counties and other municipalities).

[7] This description of the final rules is based on a question and answers document and a press release outlining the rule issued by the CFTC on January 12, 2012. A copy of the final rule itself was not available.

[8] A swap dealer acts as an adviser to a special entity when it recommends a swap or trading strategy involving a sway that is tailored to the particular needs of the special entity.

[9] Section 975 of the Dodd-Frank Act defines "municipal adviser" to include, among others and subject to certain exclusions, any person that provides advice to or on behalf of a municipal entity with respect to municipal financial products, including municipal derivatives. The Municipal Securities Rulemaking Board has begun the rulemaking process with respect to the fiduciary and other obligations of municipal advisers to their municipal entity clients.

End Notes for Appendix II

[1] MSRB currently collects information on all municipal securities transactions within 15 minutes of the trade through RTRS, which began operating on January 31, 2005. Data from January 1, 2005, through January 30, 2005, were collected by MSRB on all municipal securities transactions the day after the trade occurred via the Trade Reporting System.

[2] MSRB data does not identify the kind of investor involved in a trade; we therefore use trade size as a proxy to indicate the kind of investor.

[3] We measured days since issuance as the trade date minus the dated date. The dated date is the date of an issue from which interest on the issue usually starts to accrue, even though the issue may actually be delivered at some later date. We use the dated date as our proxy for the date a bond is issued, because the delivery date—the date that is considered the issuance date in a municipal securities primary offering—was not included in our dataset. We found that other researchers have used the dated date as a proxy for the date a bond is issued. We also found that trades that take place prior to the dated date tend to settle on or after the dated date—about 70 percent or more settle on the dated date and more than 99 percent settle on or after the dated date. This finding is consistent with the practice of trades that occur prior to the date a bond is issued, settling on the date a bond is issued. Thus, we believe using the dated date as a proxy for the date a bond is issued is reasonable.

[4] The American Economic Association provides EconLit, an electronic bibliography of economics literature, including journal articles and working papers; JSTOR is a nonprofit service that offers a digital archive of academic journals; the NBER Working Paper Series is a database of working papers submitted by NBER researchers; and SSRN publishes abstracts and working papers submitted by researchers, journals, publishers and institutions.

[5] When we reviewed the FINRA examinations, we discovered that 1 of the examinations we had selected for a G-30 violation alone also included a G-14 violation. Thus, we actually reviewed 12 examinations with both a G-14 and a G-30 violation.

[6] Because OCC, FDIC, and the Federal Reserve identified few examinations with Rule G14 violations and no examinations with G-30 violations, we expanded our sample to examinations with other violations (for example, MSRB Rule G-27 on supervision). This allowed us to see more examination reports and observe how these regulators conducted their examinations in general. We reviewed a combined total of 15 examination reports from these regulators.

[7] When we requested the OCIE examinations in March 2011, we had not yet narrowed our scope to Rules G-30 and G-14. Therefore, we requested and reviewed examinations that had violations of several other MSRB rules. The number of examinations we reviewed that involved G-30 or G-14 violations were 13 and 26, respectively.

[8] The fixed-income inspections we reviewed were of the National Association of Securities Dealers (NASD), which formerly acted as the SRO for broker-dealers. In July 2007, NASD assumed the broker-dealer regulatory functions of the New York Stock Exchange and became FINRA.

End Notes for Appendix III

[1] According to market participants, most trades by individual investors are $100,000 or less, while most trades by institutional investors are more than $1 million. MSRB data do not

identify the kind of investor involved in a trade; therefore, we use trade size as a proxy for the kind of investor.

[2] See appendix II for additional information on our methodology for constructing the data used in our analyses.

[3] The inside spread is the difference between the lowest trade price on a dealer sale and the highest trade price on a dealer purchase as a percentage of the highest trade price on a dealer purchase.

[4] The mean spread is the difference between the mean trade price on a dealer sale and the mean trade price on a dealer purchase as a percentage of the mean trade price on a dealer purchase.

[5] The outside spread is the difference between the highest trade price on a dealer sale and the lowest trade price on a dealer purchase as a percentage of the lowest trade price on a dealer purchase.

End Notes for Appendix IV

[1] MSRB Rule G-37 prohibits municipal securities dealers from engaging in municipal securities business with issuers if certain political contributions have been made to officials of such issuers. It also requires them to disclose certain political contributions to MSRB to allow for regulatory and public scrutiny. Political contribution disclosure information is available at www.msrb.org.

[2] http://emma.msrb.org/.

[3] Prior to the Transparency Programs, MSRB operated the Municipal Securities Information Library (MSIL), which collected, stored, and provided subscription access to some municipal securities market information, including issuer official statements, advance refunding documents, and a limited number of material event notices through a continuing disclosure subsystem of MSIL (CDINet). MSIL also maintained files for public access to information about political contributions and municipal securities business submitted by municipal securities dealers active in the new issue market. In addition, MSRB operated the Trade Reporting System (TRS), which provided next-day public dissemination of reported municipal securities trades. In January 2005, MSRB replaced the TRS system with the Real-Time Transaction Reporting System. The data in that system were available only to subscribers, although the subscription feed data were made available to the public through the InvestingInBonds.com website of The Bond Market Association (now known as the Securities Industry and Financial Markets Association). When MSRB launched the EMMA website in 2008 as a pilot, MSRB began making its official statements and advanced refunding documents collected through MSIL and trade prices collected through RTRS publicly available through the EMMA website. In 2009 MSRB formally initiated the Primary Market Disclosure Program (replacing most elements of MSIL) and the Transaction Data Program (incorporating RTRS), the Short-Term Disclosure Program, and the Continuing Disclosure Program (replacing CDINet) and continued to provide access to information on political contributions through the Political Contribution Disclosure Program.

[4] MSRB also increased other fees and assessments in fiscal years 2009 and 2010, but MSRB staff do not anticipate that these will generate significant sources of revenue to mitigate the costs of the Transparency Programs. These actions included amending its underwriting

assessment to remove certain exemptions and to establish a single uniform assessment rate of $0.03 per $1,000 par value, increasing its annual registration fee from $300 to $500 for dealers, adding a new fee to be assessed on individuals taking certain professional qualifications examinations, and increasing subscription fees to its real-time feeds of trade data and disclosure documents associated with new and existing municipal security issues.

End Notes for Appendix VI

[1] On December 16, 2011, SEC approved a MSRB proposed rule change that included an amendment to MSRB Rule G-16, which had required FINRA and the federal banking regulators to examine broker-dealers at least once every 2 calendar years to determine their compliance with all applicable MSRB rules, as well as other SEC rules and regulations. The amended rule allows for up to a 4-year examination cycle for FINRA member firms, consistent with FINRA's existing requirement for examination cycles for all other FINRA members. According to MSRB, broker-dealer firms that present higher risks would be examined on an annual basis, while other firms would be examined every 2 to 4 years, depending on the risks they presented. Cycle examination frequencies for FINRA member broker-dealer firms would be reassessed at least on an annual basis.

[2] FINRA also runs surveillance programs to identify other potential trade reporting issues, such as large (over a certain dollar amount) late reported trades, negative yields, excessive commissions, or unusual trade times, among other issues.

In: Municipal Securities
Editors: A. Harper and F. G. Lawson
ISBN: 978-1-62257-820-7

Chapter 2

MUNICIPAL SECURITIES: OPTIONS FOR IMPROVING CONTINUING DISCLOSURE*

The United States Government Accountability Office

ABBREVIATIONS

CUSIP	Committee on Uniform Security Identification Procedures
EMMA	Electronic Municipal Markets Access
FASB	Financial Accounting Standards Board
FINRA	Financial Industry Regulatory Authority
GAAP	generally accepted accounting principles
GASB	Governmental Accounting Standards Board
MSRB	Municipal Securities Rulemaking Board
SEC	Securities and Exchange Commission
SRO	self-regulatory organization

WHY GAO DID THIS STUDY

Municipal securities are debt instruments that state and local governments issue to finance diverse public projects. As of March 31, 2012, individual

* This is an edited, reformatted and augmented version of The United States Government Accountability Office publication, Report to Congressional Requesters GAO-12-698, dated July 2012.

investors held up to 75 percent of the total value of municipal securities outstanding. These securities are exempt from certain federal disclosure requirements applicable to other securities sold publicly. Disclosure provided in the primary market, where these securities are issued, generally consists of official statements. Continuing disclosure is information provided in the secondary market, where these securities are bought and sold after issuance. The Dodd-Frank Wall Street Reform and Consumer Protection Act required GAO to review the information issuers of municipal securities must disclose for the benefit of investors.

This report addresses (1) the extent to which information currently provided on municipal securities is useful for investors and the extent to which existing regulations reflect principles for effective disclosure, and (2) options for improving the information issuers disclose to investors of municipal securities. To conduct this work, GAO reviewed disclosure rules and compared them with principles for effective disclosure cited by SEC and the International Organization of Securities Commissions, surveyed selected experts and market participants, and interviewed issuers.

GAO provided a draft of this report to SEC, MSRB, and the Financial Industry Regulatory Authority (FINRA). SEC and MSRB provided technical comments, which GAO incorporated, as appropriate. FINRA did not provide comments.

What GAO Found

Market participants indicated that primary market disclosure for municipal securities—official statements—generally provides useful information, but investors and market participants cited a number of limitations to continuing disclosures. The most frequently cited limitations were timeliness, frequency, and completeness. For example, investors and other market participants said that issuers do not always provide all the financial information, event notices, or other information they pledged to provide for the lifetime of a security. While GAO's analysis of current regulatory requirements for municipal securities disclosure found that they largely reflected the seven principles of effective disclosure, regulators and market participants said that there are some limitations on the enforceability and efficiency of the regulations. However, the effect of these limitations on individual investors largely is unknown because limited information exists about the extent to which individual investors use disclosures to make investment decisions. Nevertheless, regulators remain concerned about this market, in part due to its size and the participation of individual investors.

As discussed below, the Securities and Exchange Commission (SEC) and Municipal Securities Rulemaking Board (MSRB) have been taking or plan to take actions to improve disclosure.

Experts and market participant groups GAO surveyed suggested options for improving disclosure, some of which would require statutory changes while others could be achieved within the existing regulatory framework. One suggested statutory change was the repeal of the Tower Amendment, which some experts believed would allow federal regulators to directly require issuers to make disclosures, but SEC and MSRB staff did not agree. The Tower Amendment prohibits SEC and MSRB from requiring issuers of municipal securities to file certain materials with them. While MSRB and SEC staff said that repealing the Tower Amendment would remove the prohibitions on requiring issuers to file certain materials with them, they noted that it would have no real effect on what they can require issuers to disclose because municipal issuers are exempt from SEC registration and MSRB does not otherwise have affirmative authority to regulate municipal issuers. Other suggestions from experts and market participant groups requiring statutory changes included mandating accounting standards and requiring the submission of financial information at intervals more frequent than annually. Experts and market participant groups suggested other options to improve disclosure that could be achieved within the existing regulatory framework, including further improving and promoting MSRB's Electronic Municipal Market Access (EMMA) system, which since July 2009 has served as the official central repository for disclosures about municipal securities. While experts and market participants said that EMMA had greatly improved their access to information on municipal securities, many suggested that further enhancements to EMMA would increase the usefulness of the system to investors and issuers. MSRB issued a plan in January 2012 to improve EMMA and recently has taken steps to enhance EMMA's functionality. Further, SEC staff indicated their plan to release a staff report in 2012 to include recommendations on measures to improve primary and secondary market disclosure practices, market practices, and associated regulation.

July 19, 2012
The Honorable Tim Johnson
Chairman

The Honorable Richard C. Shelby
Ranking Member
Committee on Banking, Housing, and Urban Affairs
United States Senate

The Honorable Spencer Bachus
Chairman
The Honorable Barney Frank Ranking Member
Committee on Financial Services House of Representatives

Municipal securities are debt instruments that state and local governments issue to finance transportation, housing, hospitals, education, and other diverse public projects.[1] The value of municipal securities outstanding was an estimated $3.7 trillion as of March 31, 2012, with individuals (also known as retail investors) holding 50 percent of the total outstanding directly, such as through purchases from broker-dealers, and up to another 25 percent indirectly through investment funds.[2] There are approximately 51,000 state and local government issuers of municipal securities and the number of separate outstanding municipal securities is estimated to be more than 1.3 million, according to information cited by the Securities and Exchange Commission (SEC).[3]

State and local governments account for 80 percent of the total outstanding.[4] Of the remaining 20 percent, corporate conduit borrowers (public and privately held companies) account for approximately 13 percent and nonprofit conduit borrowers (such as schools, health care providers, and nonprofit housing developers) account for approximately 7 percent.[5]

Concerns have been raised about whether investors—particularly retail investors—have access to enough information about municipal securities to make informed investment decisions. Some professional analysts also believe investors may be at heightened risk as states, municipalities, and other entities that issue debt struggle with the aftermath of the recent financial crisis and growing pension obligations. While the federal securities laws generally require certain disclosure in connection with the issuance of securities, Congress exempted municipal securities from the registration and periodic reporting provisions of the federal securities laws, but not the antifraud provisions. Furthermore, SEC and the Municipal Securities Rulemaking Board (MSRB) are not authorized to require issuers of municipal securities to file certain materials.[6] The specific prohibitions differ for each regulator, pursuant to provisions of the Securities Acts Amendments of 1975, generally known as the Tower Amendment.[7]

The Dodd-Frank Wall Street Reform and Consumer Protection Act (Dodd-Frank Act) directs us to conduct a study and review of the disclosure required to be made by issuers of municipal securities.[8] This report addresses (1) the extent to which information currently provided on municipal securities is useful and the extent to which existing regulation reflects principles for effective disclosure, and (2) options for improving the information issuers disclose to investors of municipal securities, and the related benefits and challenges of these options.

To describe the extent to which information is useful for investors and the extent to which existing regulations reflect principles for effective disclosure, we reviewed SEC and MSRB rules, SEC and MSRB staff reports for improving disclosures, and comment letters submitted to SEC regarding its study of the municipal securities market. We reviewed disclosure information in the Electronic Municipal Market Access (EMMA) system, the official central repository for disclosures about municipal securities. We compared disclosure regulations with principles for effective disclosure from the International Organization of Securities Commissions (*Principles for Ongoing Disclosure and Material Development Reporting by Listed Entities*) and SEC's Plain English Handbook. We reviewed independent and academic studies on the usefulness of disclosure information, and data on municipal securities defaults from independent research firms and rating agencies to understand the risks to investors of municipal securities. We worked through the American Association of Individual Investors to identify and interview 12 retail investors with diverse investment experience with municipal securities. For more perspectives of individual investors, we reviewed transcripts of SEC hearings on the state of the municipal securities market held in 2010 and 2011 and reviewed a study conducted for SEC on the usefulness of SEC-mandated disclosure documents. We also conducted a case study of 14 issuances and made observations about EMMA and the usefulness of the disclosures from the individual investors' points of view. We also interviewed institutional investors (including representatives of eight investment companies), professional analysts, an independent research firm, and groups representing market participants, including broker-dealers, bond lawyers, and municipal advisors. We interviewed staff of federal and state regulators, self-regulatory organizations (SRO), and associations, including SEC, MSRB, the Financial Industry Regulatory Authority (FINRA), and the North American Securities Administrators Association.[9]

To identify options for improving the information issuers disclose to investors, we reviewed securities laws, regulations, and guidance. We also reviewed SEC and FINRA examination manuals for SEC Rule 15c2- 12, which establishes requirements for the underwriters of municipal securities, and reviewed data on examinations that found violations of the rule. [10] Furthermore, we surveyed experts and groups representing issuers and other market participants, such as municipal advisors, broker-dealers, and professional analysts. We used a nonprobability sampling method to identify and select experts by obtaining referrals from other market participants, experts, and regulators. Although our results are not generalizable, our survey covered a diverse group of experts and market participant groups with broad and differing perspectives. We administered the survey to 26 experts and 29 market participant groups and received responses from 21 experts and 21 groups. To identify the benefits and challenges of these options, we interviewed issuers in three groups representing (1) large and frequent issuers, (2) small and infrequent issuers, and (3) conduit issuers. To provide information about options for improving disclosure information and related benefits and challenges, we also drew on the interviews we conducted with investors, regulators, and market participants.

We conducted this performance audit from June 2011 to July 2012 in accordance with generally accepted government auditing standards. Those standards require that we plan and perform the audit to obtain sufficient, appropriate evidence to provide a reasonable basis for our findings and conclusions based on our audit objectives. We believe that the evidence obtained provides a reasonable basis for our findings and conclusions based on our audit objectives. Appendix I provides a more detailed description of our scope and methodology.

BACKGROUND

SEC and MSRB are the primary entities that have authority at the federal level with respect to disclosure to investors in municipal securities. In the context of municipal securities, SEC interprets and enforces the federal securities laws, including by adopting rules and enforcing antifraud provisions; maintaining regimes for the registration, compliance, inspection, and education of broker-dealers, investment advisers, and municipal advisors; and providing general educational materials for investors about investing in municipal securities.[11] SEC also oversees MSRB and FINRA. MSRB maintains an online repository of information (that is, EMMA) to promote market transparency, for example, by providing access to primary market and continuing disclosures and information about trade pricing.[12] MSRB also provides educational materials to investors and issuers of municipal securities. MSRB regulates brokers, dealers, municipal securities dealers, and municipal advisors in the municipal securities market by adopting rules governing their conduct, which are subject to SEC approval. However, MSRB does not have authority to enforce these rules or examine entities for compliance with these rules. Rather, SEC, FINRA, and bank regulators enforce MSRB rules and conduct compliance examinations.[13]

The Tower Amendment prohibits SEC and MSRB from directly requiring state and local governments to submit information to them prior to sale. Specifically, SEC and MSRB cannot require issuers to file any information with them prior to any sale, and MSRB also cannot require issuers to provide them or investors with any information either pre- or postsale. Furthermore, the Securities Act of 1933 exempts the securities that state and local governments issue from registration with SEC. Securities of state and local governments also are exempt from the periodic disclosure requirements of the Exchange Act of 1934. According to a 1975 Senate report, congressional reasons for the decision to continue to limit direct regulation of issuers when the 1975 amendments to the securities acts were enacted included respect for the rights of state governments to access the capital markets, concerns about the costs of regulation for state and local government issuers, and the perceived lack of abuses in the municipal market that would justify such an incursion on the states' prerogatives.[14]

While federal regulators are prohibited from directly requiring issuers to file presale information on municipal securities, SEC has adopted rules—applicable to broker-dealers acting as underwriters—that relate to primary market and continuing disclosures.[15] More specifically, using its authority over broker-dealers and its broad authority to prevent fraud in connection with the offer, purchase, or sale of securities, SEC adopted Rule 15c2-12 in 1989. The rule established disclosure requirements related to municipal securities in response to the need SEC found for increased transparency.[16] This rule and accompanying guidance obligates underwriters of municipal securities to obtain and review issuers' official statements (typically prepared by issuers or their advisors) and provide them to investors.[17] In addition, the rule was amended in 1995 to require underwriters to reasonably determine that issuers have entered into a written continuing disclosure agreement for the benefit of municipal securities holders to provide (1) annual financial information and operating data of the type included in the official statement and when and if available, audited financial statements, and (2) notices of certain material events. Beginning in 2009, issuers have been obligated by the agreement to provide the continuing disclosure information and data to EMMA (either directly or by engaging a third-party dissemination agent to submit such information and data on their behalf). For a comparison of key federal disclosure requirements for publicly offered municipal and corporate securities, see appendix II.

Investors access disclosure information in EMMA at no cost through a website maintained by MSRB, which created the system in 2008 primarily to benefit retail investors, also known as individual investors. 18 Documents available in EMMA include official statements (that is, information provided to investors at the initial offering) that underwriters must submit. EMMA also makes available postsale information submitted by issuers or their dissemination agents, including the annual reports of financial information, notices of certain events, and certain other categories of information that issuers may voluntarily provide. The events that issuers (or other obligated persons) must agree to provide notices of include principal and interest payment delinquencies; unscheduled draws on debt service reserves reflecting financial difficulties; and bankruptcy,

insolvency, receivership and similar events.[19] MSRB allows issuers to voluntarily submit to EMMA on a continuing basis any other types of financial, operating, or event-based information, including (but not limited to) information about bank loans, quarterly or monthly financial information, consultant reports, and capital or other financing plans. According to MSRB, users may conduct searches of issuances on EMMA using one or more of the following parameters: Committee on Uniform Security Identification Procedures (CUSIP) number, issuer name, issue description, obligated person name, state, maturity date, date of issuance, interest rate, and ratings. EMMA provides additional parameters to search for continuing disclosure documents and other information available through EMMA, including trade information.

INVESTORS AND MARKET PARTICIPANTS CITED LIMITATIONS OF CONTINUING DISCLOSURES

Many market participants told us that primary market disclosure for municipal securities investors is generally useful. However, investors and market participants with whom we spoke frequently cited limitations to continuing disclosure, including the timeliness of annual financial information, the frequency with which information is provided, and incomplete information. Our analysis found that current regulatory requirements for municipal securities disclosure broadly reflect the seven principles of effective disclosure that were developed by the International Organization of Securities Commissions and certain plain English principles developed by SEC. However, regulators and market participants indicated that, in practice, limitations exist in the current regulatory scheme. Further, the effect on individual investors of limitations to disclosure is largely unknown.

Investors and Market Participants Most Commonly Cited Timeliness, Frequency, and Completeness as Disclosure Limitations

Many market participants told us primary market disclosure is generally useful for investors and EMMA has improved investor and market participants' ability to access disclosure documents, but investors and market participants have identified limitations to disclosure. According to MSRB officials, participants in the municipal securities market generally acknowledge that primary market disclosure—official statements— contains the material facts an investor needs to know about an issuer and a security.[20] Investors and market participants such as groups representing investment companies, bond lawyers, and broker-dealers also have indicated that the information provided at the time of issuance is comprehensive. Additionally, most market participant groups with whom we spoke said that MSRB's EMMA website has greatly improved public access to disclosure compared with the prior system for obtaining disclosure documents.[21] Several market participants said that having a central repository for disclosure documents has made finding information easier and more efficient. In addition, one market participant noted that EMMA increased access to information by allowing investors to receive disclosures for free.

However, investors and other market participants cited limitations to the information provided in continuing disclosures. The most frequently cited limitations to the usefulness of this information were: the timeliness of annual financial information, the frequency with which issuers and other obligated persons provided information, and the completeness of the information provided in accordance with the continuing disclosure agreement. Individual investors also frequently cited the readability of disclosures as a limitation.

- Timeliness—According to investors and other market participants, issuers release annual financial information too long after the end of their fiscal years for the information to be useful in making investment decisions. A Governmental Accounting Standards Board (GASB) study of audited annual financial reports prepared in accordance with generally accepted accounting principles (GAAP) for state and local governments provided for fiscal years ending in 2006, 2007, and 2008 found that the average time frame for issuing the reports varied by type and size of government. For example, issuance time frames averaged from 126 days after the end of the fiscal year for large special districts to 244 days for small counties.[22] Similarly, according to National Association of State Comptrollers data, in fiscal year 2010 states took an average of 198 days to complete their comprehensive annual financial reports. Also, in our case study of disclosures for 14 securities in EMMA that were issued in 2009, our analysis found that the number of days after the end of the fiscal year in which issuers or obligated persons provided annual financial information to EMMA varied. Annual financial information for a nonprofit hospital system was provided 55 days after the end of a fiscal year, while annual financial information for a general obligation security issued by a school district was provided 257 days after the end of a fiscal year. Several investors and market participants said that filings provided well after the end of the fiscal year limit the information's usefulness. The GASB study found similar sentiments: less than 9 percent of survey respondents—who represented a range of users of financial information—considered information received 6 months after the end of the fiscal year to be very useful.[23] Three market participants further indicated that untimely information was particularly worrisome for investors at a time when state and local governments have been facing credit stress. Moreover, evidence indicates that issuers have not always met the time frames by which they agreed to provide annual information. For example, a study by the California Debt and Investment Advisory Commission of certain securities issued in California from 2005 to 2009 found 11 percent filed more than 30 days after the agreed-upon date.[24]

- Frequency—Investors and other market participants also said that receiving financial information annually was not sufficient to monitor the financial condition of an issuer. An individual investor with whom we spoke and a professional analyst both noted that because disclosures generally are provided annually, investors often must learn important information about the current financial condition of an issuer from external sources such as newspaper articles. For instance, the individual investor told us that he may read in the newspaper that a town that issued securities was having budget problems; however, this information would not be disclosed to investors until the financial statements for the fiscal year were released at some point during the following year. A few market participants indicated that obtaining information more frequently was especially important for investors during times of economic stress. Information that investors and other market participants indicated would be useful to receive between annual financial statements included unaudited quarterly financial reports, cash-flow reports, year-to-date budget updates, and tax revenue information. This type of information is not routinely submitted to EMMA on a voluntary basis. According to MSRB data, in 2011 EMMA received 8,290 submissions categorized as quarterly or monthly financial information (which represents 6 percent of all continuing disclosure documents submitted) and 358 submissions categorized as interim, additional financial information, or operating data. Similarly, quarterly or monthly financial information was available in EMMA for 5 of the 14 securities in our case study.
- Completeness—Investors and other market participants said that issuers do not always provide all of the financial information, event notices, or other information they agreed to provide in a continuing disclosure agreement for the lifetime of a security. For example, three market participants told us that issuers and obligated persons did not always file the annual financial information that they agreed to provide. Our case study of disclosures for 14 securities in EMMA identified similar issues in a few cases. In particular, our analysis found that 2 securities—a 2009 general obligation security for a small issuer and a 2009 conduit offering with a publicly traded corporation as the obligated person—had no financial or other continuing disclosures as of May 2012. In addition, a few market participants indicated that filings of event notices can be delayed significantly or

that event notices may never be filed. For instance, one market participant said that he had noted cases in which issuers failed to report unscheduled draws on debt service or adverse tax opinions. Such lapses in reporting may also go undetected. As one market participant and a FINRA official noted, an investor or regulator may not be able to ascertain if a reportable event had occurred unless an event notice was filed with EMMA. Finally, a few market participants told us that issuers may provide all of the information they agreed to provide for the first few years after a security was issued, but afterwards fail to provide some of the information—for instance, tax data or operating information.

- Readability—Individual investors commonly cited concerns about the readability of disclosure documents.[25] Four of the 12 individual investors with whom we spoke said that disclosure documents were not easy to read or understand. Furthermore, most individual investors with whom we spoke said that they generally had limited time to decide whether to buy a security, leaving them little time to research a security.[26] Several individual investors and market participants said that disclosures were difficult to understand because they contained extensive legal or technical terminology and complex information. In addition, two of the individual investors with whom we spoke noted that the information for which they looked was "buried" in the disclosure documents and not easy to find.
- To a lesser extent, investors and other market participants identified additional limitations—including the lack of standardization and limitations of EMMA—to the usefulness of disclosure. Several market participants said that the lack of standardization of disclosure across different issuers impeded their ability to compare issuances. MSRB also stated in a comment letter to SEC in 2011 that many investors have told MSRB that the lack of standardization in disclosure is a problem.[27] MSRB indicated that elements that market participants would like to see standardized included the use of bond proceeds and some basic information, such as the manner of reporting the name of the issuer or other obligated person and information on the source of repayment. Two market participants also told us standardization of accounting methods and the format of disclosures would make disclosures more useful. Also, investors and other market participants described several aspects of EMMA that limited its usefulness. Several market participants noted that the ability to search

for issuances was limited, especially if users did not have the CUSIP number for the issuance in which they were interested.[28] Two market participants noted that continuing disclosures sometimes were categorized incorrectly by the issuer at submission to EMMA and one said that issuers may not submit disclosures for all issuances to which they applied.

Current Regulations Broadly Reflect Disclosure Principles but Some Limitations Exist

We compared requirements for continuing disclosure in SEC Rule 15c2-12 and SEC's antifraud authorities with principles for effective disclosure that were developed by an international organization of securities commissions, which included SEC, and certain plain English principles developed by SEC.[29] These principles include allocation of accountability, continuing disclosure obligation, disclosure criteria, dissemination of information, equal treatment of disclosure, timeliness, and use of plain English in official statements (see app. III for the comparison of the principles and municipal securities disclosure requirements). We found that current regulations broadly reflect the seven principles of effective disclosure. However, regulators and market participants have indicated that, in practice, limitations exist in the current regulatory scheme, including the areas of enforceability, content, and efficiency. In particular, they noted the following:

- Allocation of accountability—Although security holders may enforce continuing disclosure agreements by bringing suit against the issuer or obligated person, SEC staff told us that they were not aware of any public statements about any such lawsuits having occurred. Also, two market participants noted that market participants other than investors directly holding a security have no remediation should an issuer or obligated person not provide disclosure. SEC and MSRB cannot enforce continuing disclosure agreements. In a comment letter to SEC in 2011, MSRB stated that because Rule 15c2-12 does not impose penalties for noncompliance with continuing disclosure agreements, there is limited accountability for those issuers or obligated persons that do not provide the information.[30] In addition, various regulatory incentives that could encourage issuers to comply with their agreements have limitations, according to regulators and market participants. For example, regulatory requirements to disclose at issuance failure to comply with prior continuing disclosure agreements only may work as an incentive to encourage issuers to make required disclosures if they anticipate issuing a new security in the future. Moreover, SEC staff and two market participants indicated that even if issuers anticipated issuing a future security they might not be sufficiently incentivized to keep up with their disclosure obligations between issuances, as some issuers may only go to market with a new issuance from every 3 to 5 years.[31] There are other reasons why issuers may not keep up with continuing disclosure responsibilities between issuances. A few market participants who work with issuers to help prepare disclosures told us that some issuers face challenges in complying with their continuing disclosure agreements because of a lack of awareness or understanding of their disclosure responsibilities, which members of one market participant group said can be due to staff turnover and competing priorities in times of budgetary challenges. Two small issuers with whom we spoke said that they do not have staff dedicated to issuing and monitoring debt, which presents a challenge in preparing disclosures.

- Continuing disclosure obligation—As a condition of an underwriting, an underwriter must reasonably determine that issuers or obligated persons have agreed to provide certain information on a continuing basis. However, this requirement is placed on the underwriter, not directly on the issuer of the security. Regulators and market participants have noted that this requirement on the underwriter is inefficient for several reasons. For example, representatives of two market participant groups told us that an underwriter often does not have an opportunity to influence the content of a continuing disclosure agreement before an issuance, although it is the underwriter's responsibility to ensure the agreement specifies that all required information will be provided. Also, FINRA staff noted that should an issuer or obligated person not provide continuing disclosure information after a security is issued, the underwriter has no means to compel them to do so. Furthermore, representatives of two market participant groups and a former regulator have indicated that a disproportionate amount of the regulatory burden for municipal disclosure falls on underwriters. In addition, Rule 15c2-12 does not expressly require underwriters to document how they comply with requirements to reasonably determine that the issuer or obligated person agreed to provide continuing disclosures and that they are likely to comply with their continuing disclosure agreement. SEC staff said that without this documentation, it may be difficult for an underwriter to demonstrate that it met its obligations.

- Timeliness—Although Rule 15c2-12 requires, as a condition of an underwriting, that an underwriter must reasonably determine that issuers or obligated persons have specified a date by which they agreed to provide the annual financial report, it does not specify what that date should be. Therefore, issuers and obligated persons may provide annual financial information months after the close of the fiscal year.
- Use of plain English—Regulations do not require the use of plain English in municipal securities' official statements or other disclosure documents.

SEC recognizes some of these limitations and has taken recent actions to improve the timeliness and completeness of continuing disclosures. Specifically, in June 2010, SEC amended Rule 15c2-12 and issued interpretive guidance to

- specify that event notices be submitted to EMMA in a timely manner not in excess of 10 business days of the occurrence of the underlying event, rather than merely "in a timely manner" as was previously required;
- remove the general materiality condition for determining whether notice of an event is to be submitted to EMMA—thereby, requiring that notification be provided for certain events when they occur regardless of whether they are determined to be material (including principal and interest payment delinquencies, and unscheduled draws on debt service reserves reflecting financial difficulties, among others), while adding separately a materiality condition to select events (including nonpayment-related defaults and bond calls);
- increase the number of events for which notice must be provided;
- remove an exemption from reporting disclosure information for certain variable-rate securities; and
- reaffirm its previous interpretation that underwriters must form a reasonable belief in the accuracy and completeness of representations made by issuers or other obligated persons in disclosures as a basis for

recommending the securities, including making a reasonable determination that the issuer will likely provide the continuing disclosure information it agreed to provide.[32]

Effect of Limitations of Disclosure Regulations on Individual Investors Largely Is Unknown

The risk posed to investors by the limitations of disclosure regulations cited by market participants is largely unknown because (1) there is limited information about the extent to which investors use disclosures to make investment decisions, (2) there is limited information about the extent to which disclosure limitations about which investors were concerned actually have occurred, and (3) there is a low incidence of defaults and other characteristics of the municipal market that mitigate investor risk. Nevertheless, SEC and MSRB have continuing concerns about disclosure in the municipal market.

There is limited information about the extent to which individual investors in municipal securities use disclosures to make investment decisions. Regulators and market participants with whom we spoke did not have overall information on the extent to which individual investors in municipal securities rely on disclosures in making their investment decisions. However, anecdotal evidence suggests that individual investors' reliance on disclosures could be limited. For example, 5 of the 12 individual investors with whom we spoke said that they relied solely on their broker-dealers' advice when making an investment decision, while the others said that they conducted their own research into securities. Of the 5 investors who said they relied solely on their broker-dealers' advice, 2 indicated that they did not rely on disclosures because of the difficulty of understanding them. Similarly, a 2008 SEC study of investor usage of disclosure documents for stocks, bonds, and mutual funds found that only 2 percent of investors surveyed cited SEC-mandated disclosure documents—prospectuses and annual reports—as the most important source of investment information.[33] Rather, surveyed investors most frequently cited financial advisors or brokers as the most important source of investment information.[34] Although the SEC study did not focus on municipal securities, some of the investors surveyed also may have invested in these types of securities. More importantly, the study provides a general indication of investors' usage of disclosure documents and other sources of information. Many individual investors with whom we spoke also said that a security's credit rating has been a main factor in making investment decisions. However, several of these investors told us that they have less faith in credit ratings than they did before the financial crisis, potentially making disclosure information a more important factor in their future investment decisions.

There is also limited information on the extent to which events relating to limitations to disclosure cited by investors—such as issuers and other obligated persons failing to submit information or submitting information late—have occurred. MSRB has limited ability to track issuances with missing or late disclosure for several reasons. For example, MSRB reported that in 2011 it received 1,879 required notices of failure to provide annual financial information; however, MSRB staff told us that they could not reliably determine the universe of issuances in EMMA for which annual financial information was required.[35] This is because EMMA did not have the capability to easily or systematically differentiate between securities that should have disclosure submissions and those that are exempt from SEC Rule 15c2-12, according to MSRB staff.[36] In addition, it is difficult for MSRB or others to develop reliable information about issuer compliance with their continuing disclosure agreements for the universe of outstanding issuances because the structure of continuing disclosure obligations can vary by issuance, making compliance with continuing disclosure agreements difficult to systematically identify and track. As a result, there is limited information on the extent of the problems.

Table 1. Cumulative Average Default Rates for Municipal and Corporate Issuers (in Percentages), as of Year-end 2011

	Standard & Poor's			Moody's Investors Service		
	1 year	5 years	10 years	1 year	5 years	10 years
U.S. municipal issuers	0.02	0.10	0.17	0.01	0.07	0.13
Global corporate issuers	1.57	6.58	9.83	1.61	7.24	11.18

Source: GAO analysis of data from Standard & Poor's and Moody's Investors Service.

Note: Default rates are cumulative average default rates for corporate and municipal debt issuers rated by each rating agency within 1, 5, and 10 years and indicate the estimated likelihood that an issuer with an outstanding rating will default in 1, 5, and 10 years, respectively. Different rating agencies may use different sets of issuers to calculate default rates. We used data from Standard & Poor's and Moody's Investors Service to compare default rates for U.S. municipal issuers and global corporate issuers by each rating agency. We assessed the reliability of these data and found them to be reliable for this purpose.

The low levels of defaults on municipal securities and other characteristics of the municipal securities market also make it difficult to determine the importance of disclosure documents as a means of investor protection. Long-term default rates associated with rated municipal securities have been less than 1 percent, which is significantly lower than long-term default rates for rated corporate debt securities (see table 1).[37] In addition, municipal bankruptcy filings historically have been rare compared with bankruptcy filings by businesses. For 1991 through 2009, 177 municipalities filed for bankruptcy. In contrast, more than 49,000 businesses filed for bankruptcy in the 12-month period ending March 31, 2009.[38]

In addition, state and local government issuers have a strong incentive to meet their payment obligations because issuances of municipal securities constitute an important tool to finance critical projects, and defaults may hinder their ability to issue future securities and may adversely affect other issuers of municipal securities in the surrounding area. Defaulted municipal securities also have a relatively high recovery rate for investors compared to corporate securities, according to two rating agencies—with one reporting a recovery rate of 67 percent for municipal securities compared with 40 percent for corporate securities.[39] Some states also have mechanisms intended to address financial crises, allowing for state intervention into a local government's finances.[40] Finally, 30 states have laws that give holders of general-obligation and certain other securities issued by municipalities within their states first rights to repayment from certain revenue streams, even during bankruptcy.[41]

Nevertheless, SEC and MSRB have expressed continuing concerns about municipal securities disclosure due to individual investors constituting a significant portion of the market, the size of the market, default risk, and incomplete disclosure. SEC staff told us that disclosure by municipal issuers should be improved in general as it relates to the primary market and continuing disclosure.42 In rulemakings, SEC staff have noted concern about the size of the municipal securities market and that, while defaults of municipal securities are rare, they do occur. Furthermore, the significant pressure on state and local government budgets and the diminishment of bond insurance since the recent financial crisis have increased focus on disclosure issues, according to SEC and MSRB staff.43 MSRB staff noted in 2010 that although the municipal securities market largely weathered the 2008 financial crisis, economic conditions and financial liabilities continued to stress municipal bond issuers. SEC staff also told us that recent SEC enforcement actions highlight risks posed by pension funding obligations.44 Furthermore,

SEC and MSRB leadership have publicly voiced concerns about various aspects of the municipal securities market. Examples of their concerns include the following:

- An SEC Commissioner remarked that investors may have trouble understanding the risks associated with increasingly complex structures used by large and small municipalities.[45]
- A former SEC Chairman stated that the opacity of the municipal market was unrivaled and presented a significant threat to the U.S. economy.[46]
- An SEC Commissioner was concerned that investors might not have access to the information they needed to accurately calculate their risks when making investment decisions. She stated at an SEC field hearing on the municipal market in 2010 that municipal market investors were afforded second-class treatment compared with that afforded to investors in other securities because they could not count on receiving accurate and timely financial and other material information about their investments.[47]
- MSRB stated in a comment letter to SEC in 2011 that MSRB received complaints about some issuers' disregard for their continuing disclosure agreements and failure to provide information on time or at all.[48]

OPTIONS FOR IMPROVING DISCLOSURE INVOLVE POTENTIAL BENEFITS AND CHALLENGES

Experts and market participant groups we surveyed suggested a number of options for improving municipal securities disclosure. Some of the options would require statutory changes while others could be achieved within existing statutory authority. Each of the suggested options involves trade-offs, and market participants and the regulators' views on the efficacy of the options varied.

Our discussion of potential benefits provided to investors and potential costs of implementing these options is limited to the views of survey and interview participants.

Some Options Identified to Improve Disclosure Would Require Statutory Changes

Experts and market participant groups we surveyed suggested some options to improve disclosure that would require statutory changes. While many suggested repealing the Tower Amendment, regulators said it would have no effect on what they could require issuers to disclose. SEC staff said the Securities Act exempts municipal issuers from SEC registration requirements. MSRB does not otherwise have affirmative authority to regulate issuers. They said additional statutory changes would be needed for regulators to implement other options we identified for improving disclosure that included prescribing accounting standards, requiring time frames for annual reporting or more frequent disclosure, and requiring certain conduit borrowers to comply with corporate disclosure requirements.

Many Survey Respondents Suggested Repealing the Tower Amendment, but Regulators Said It Would Have No Effect on Disclosure

Seven of 21 experts we surveyed suggested that Congress repeal the Tower Amendment—provisions that prohibit SEC and MSRB from requiring issuers to file any information with them prior to any sale, and MSRB from requiring issuers to provide them or investors with any information pre- or postsale. Some experts believe that repealing these provisions would allow federal regulators to directly require issuers to provide continuing disclosures, and thereby address concerns about incomplete submissions or failures to meet obligations under continuing disclosure agreements, but SEC and MSRB staff did not agree and said additional changes would be needed for them to directly regulate issuers.

As noted previously, the Tower Amendment prohibits SEC and MSRB from requiring state and local governments to file presale information with them in connection with the issuance, sale, or distribution of municipal securities. MSRB is further limited by a prohibition against requiring any issuer to furnish it or any purchaser or prospective purchaser with any document or report about the issuer, except for documents and information that generally are available from a source other than the issuer. Some industry participants believe the Tower Amendment prohibits any regulation of municipal issuers, while others believe its scope is narrower and addresses only prefiling requirements. SEC staff noted that repealing the Tower Amendment would have no real effect on disclosure because of exemptions under the Securities Act. SEC and MSRB staff agreed that repealing the

Tower Amendment would remove a prohibition on requiring issuers to file presale information. However, they said such repeal would have no effect on their ability to establish disclosure requirements for issuers with respect to primary or continuing disclosures. SEC staff told us that the Securities Act provision that broadly exempts municipal securities from SEC's registration requirements means that the registration requirements applicable to corporate issuers do not apply to municipal securities offerings. In addition, the periodic reporting requirements of the Exchange Act do not apply to issuers of such municipal securities. MSRB does not otherwise have affirmative authority to regulate municipal issuers. As a result, SEC and MSRB staff told us that Congress may need to provide SEC or MSRB with affirmative authority or amend exemptions under federal securities laws to establish disclosure requirements directly on municipal securities issuers.[49]

Four market participant groups we surveyed and others (including issuers) with whom we spoke discussed potential challenges to issuers of expanding regulator authority. They expressed concern over the costs of federal regulation as well as the potential infringement on state and local government rights. According to a market participant group with whom we spoke, an increase in the costs of accessing the market could prohibit some issuers from raising capital in the public market and lead some issuers to pursue other options for raising capital, such as through private bank loans. In addition, a market participant group representing issuers said the basic tenets of federalism and the importance of federal-state comity behind the Tower Amendment were important considerations in weighing potential options for improving municipal disclosure.

While neither SEC nor MSRB had indicated to us they were seeking additional authority to regulate issuers, SEC staff indicated that additional authority would be helpful to improve disclosure by municipal issuers. Staff of each regulator had similar views on how to most appropriately use any additional authority that could be granted to regulate disclosure by municipal issuers.

- First, staff generally agreed that the securities registration regime for public companies would be inappropriate for the municipal securities market. With approximately 50,000 issuers and 1.3 million separate outstanding securities, SEC staff said the additional resources potentially needed to review and declare effective registration statements would be extensive, and an MSRB official said regulating municipal issuers would be beyond MSRB's current resource capabilities.

- Second, SEC and MSRB staff recognize that potential continuing disclosure requirements could have costs for issuers, such as small or infrequent issuers, although limited information exists on the universe of issuers, and issuers that might be affected.
- Third, SEC and MSRB staff told us broad-based or marketwide standardized disclosure would not be favorable for the municipal market. Rather, SEC staff told us disclosure requirements could be principles-based. Principles-based disclosure is an approach that would involve establishing key objectives of good reporting and providing guidance and examples to explain each objective. MSRB staff agreed that disclosure requirements should be tailored, noting that the market is highly diverse in terms of the structure of financings and the issuing community. Staff from both regulators said any disclosure requirements for municipal securities issuers would need to reflect the diversity of issuers as well as the federal interest in investor protection.
- Fourth, SEC and MSRB staff stated that regulation of municipal securities must balance investor protection and intergovernmental comity. For example, SEC staff told us any federal regulation of municipal securities disclosure should be flexible and adaptable, so that regulators could account for issues of comity and other political realities present in the municipal market.

Additional Options for Improving Disclosure Would Require Other Statutory Changes

In addition to repealing the Tower Amendment, many of the experts and market participants we surveyed identified additional options that would require statutory changes. These include prescribing accounting standards and requiring time frames for annual reporting, requiring more frequent disclosure, or requiring certain conduit borrowers to comply with corporate disclosure provisions. According to SEC and MSRB staff, Congress would need to provide SEC or MSRB with authority to implement any of these options.

Prescribe Accounting Standards

Five of 21 experts we surveyed and a market participant group with whom we spoke suggested federal regulators should prescribe accounting standards for the financial information issuers disclose in EMMA. These suggestions included that SEC should be provided authority to prescribe accounting standards or regulators should require issuers to comply with GAAP for state and local governments.[50] Additionally, three market participant groups suggested regulators should have authority to simplify GAAP standards to more efficiently meet investor needs and reduce compliance costs for issuers. According to MSRB staff, Congress could provide MSRB authority to regulate issuers and authorize accounting standards without needing to repeal the Tower Amendment. According to MSRB staff, without statutory changes, MSRB could use existing authority to prohibit broker-dealers from underwriting new securities without an issuer of such securities committing to follow GAAP or other accounting standards. However, an MSRB official also told us that approach would be less effective than directly regulating issuers, an unreasonable burden on broker-dealers, be difficult to comply with and enforce, and could be viewed as an indirect obligation for issuers.

According to an expert, a market participant group, and SEC staff with whom we spoke, standardized accounting requirements could benefit investors by facilitating comparability of financial information across different issuers and securities, and make annual financial information easier to understand, particularly for individual investors. We previously reported that many industry participants think GAAP-basis financial statements provide a fuller, more transparent picture of a government's financial position than those prepared in accordance with other bases of accounting. 51 Reporting of pension liability is one of the areas that market participants and experts we surveyed said should be improved. Appendix IV provides information on several industry-driven efforts to improve pension liability reporting in municipal securities disclosure documents.

However, according to some interview and survey participants, issuers could face challenges in complying with standardized accounting requirements. According to a market participant group and small and conduit issuers with whom we spoke, as well as 2 of 21 experts we surveyed, complying with complex and changing GAAP standards would be too costly for smaller issuers that may not have full-time accounting staff and lack technical expertise. Some issuers also told us a requirement to follow GAAP would be an unfunded mandate, particularly for small or infrequent borrowers because they would be required to invest in the staff time and expertise to prepare financial statements they would not otherwise prepare.[52] Some issuers also questioned the potential benefits to investors of mandated GAAP compliance, saying that statements that comply with GAAP provide too much irrelevant information to investors.

An MSRB official told us authority to prescribe accounting standards would be more appropriate for SEC, as such authority would be within its regulatory purview because of its oversight of the corporate market. 53 MSRB stated it had neither the expertise nor resources to determine appropriate accounting standards and likely would not support such action. An MSRB official told us that appropriate due diligence and consideration of the balance of benefits and burdens should be conducted before requiring all issuers to comply with GAAP standards because of the significant impact such a mandate could have on issuers. SEC staff told us SEC had not expressed a view on whether SEC should have authority to prescribe accounting standards used in primary and continuing municipal disclosure documents. SEC staff told us it could be desirable to require municipal issuers to use GAAP-basis accounting for their securities offerings, but it may be appropriate to first apply any requirement to the largest and most frequent municipal issuers. In 2009, an SEC Commissioner suggested that legislation could provide SEC with authority to require municipal issuers to use GAAP and recognize the financial accounting and reporting standards of an accounting standard-setting body, such as GASB, as "generally accepted."54 In a 2010 speech at a securities regulation seminar, the Commissioner identified options for improving municipal securities disclosure that SEC would examine in an ongoing review of the municipal securities market.55 They included mandating the use of uniform accounting standards, such as GAAP standards.

Require Time Frames for Annual Reporting

Four of 21 experts and 4 of 21 market participant groups we surveyed, and 2 market participant groups we interviewed, suggested that federal regulators should require issuers to submit annual financial statements and operating information on a timely basis. Suggestions included that state and local government issuers should meet a standard of 120 or 180 days, or adhere to the same standard as corporate issuers.[56] Improving timeliness could benefit the market by helping build investor confidence in a particular security or issuer and thereby increase investor demand for municipal securities, according to 3 of the market participant groups and 1 of the experts. In turn, increased demand theoretically could improve pricing and increase liquidity, but to what extent this would be the case is unknown. While SEC requires in Rule 15c2-12, as a condition of an underwriting, that an underwriter must reasonably determine that the issuer or obligated person has agreed in a continuing disclosure agreement to specify the date on which annual financial information will be provided, SEC does not have authority to enforce this aspect of the agreement.

Issuers discussed potential challenges of meeting shorter annual reporting time frames. Large issuers (including states, cities, and a county) told us a dependence on other entities—including component units of government—for information could prohibit entities that satisfy their annual reporting obligation by submitting audited financial statements from completing audited financial statements in shorter time frames.[57] A state conduit issuer said some issuers might rely on a state to reconcile Medicare payments after the close of the fiscal year before they could report GAAP-compliant financial statements. In addition, some issuers said a limited availability of auditors of governmental entities could impede issuers from complying with a mandated annual reporting time frame.[58] Some states require their local governments to use state auditors, in which case the local government might have little to no control over the timing of the audit. Other states use private-sector auditors, and several issuers told us that there is a shortage of these auditors. For example, an issuer from Wisconsin noted that major accounting firms have reduced staff resources supporting public-sector audits, and smaller auditing firms also have moved away from government audits.

MSRB staff discussed with us their perspectives on possibly requiring issuers to provide annual financial information on a timelier basis. They said the diversity of the issuer community and significant impediments to implementing such an option would need to be evaluated before putting in place such a requirement. In response to market participant concerns that information needed to make informed investment decisions is stale in many cases, MSRB recently developed features in EMMA that allow issuers, obligated persons, and parties providing disclosure upon their behalf, to voluntarily specify a time frame of 120 or 150 days for submitting annual financial information.

Require Quarterly Reporting

Three market participant groups we interviewed and 1 of 21 market participant groups we surveyed told us federal regulators should require issuers to disclose unaudited financial information on a quarterly basis in EMMA, similar to requirements for corporate issuers. According to 3 market participant groups, more frequent reporting could help provide investors with more timely, relevant information.

Four of seven large issuers and three of six small issuers told us they posted interim financial information to their websites, including unaudited quarterly financial statements and budget reports. Three other small issuers that produced interim financial reports told us they did not post such information on their websites, but could provide it to investors or others on request. Issuers that already produce interim financial information could face minimal cost to submit it to EMMA. Additionally, members of a market participant group representing issuers said unaudited interim financial information might be easier for issuers to prepare than annual audited financial reports (for issuers that fulfill their annual reporting obligation as agreed in their continuing disclosure agreement by providing audited annual financial statements) and provide investors with more current and relevant information. One market participant group representing issuers told us smaller issuers could have a greater incentive to disclose interim financial information for the benefit of investors out of competitive pressure as more issuers adopted the practice.

However, issuers and a market participant group indicated that a requirement for issuers to provide quarterly information to EMMA could be costly, would involve liability concerns, and could result in a limited presentation of financial information that excludes information on accrued assets and liabilities. Some large, small, and conduit issuers with whom we spoke said preparing interim financial information for EMMA would require additional staff resources and, with governments' limited resources, likely would result in issuers reallocating staff resources from other areas. For example, several large issuers and conduit issuers told us they and others would need to hire additional accounting staff if required to provide standardized quarterly financial reports. Large and small issuers also cited concerns about their liability under SEC's antifraud authority of posting unaudited financial information to EMMA, and a market participant group suggested that issuers would be more willing to disclose interim information if they could disclaim liability from the antifraud provisions of the federal securities laws. SEC staff told us that issuers and others cannot disclaim liability or responsibility for their disclosures under the antifraud provisions. Finally, several large and small issuers with whom we spoke and 1 of 21 market participant groups we surveyed said significant adjustments that some government entities make only at year-end to meet GAAP requirements would make it infeasible to determine an issuer's financial condition from interim financial reports, as interim information would provide an incomplete picture of an issuer's financial condition.

In a 2010 speech to the Investment Company Institute, the SEC Chairman stated that requiring periodic disclosure of financial information—such as tax revenues, expenditures, tax base changes, or pension obligations—could help improve municipal securities disclosure.[59] Further, MSRB staff told us quarterly disclosure could enable investors to better compare different types of securities, as more information would be available for comparative analyses. In addition, they said more frequent disclosure in theory could increase liquidity and improve pricing, but it would be difficult to determine to what extent, and whether, more frequent disclosure would increase liquidity and improve pricing. MSRB staff told us variation among the issuer community also constitutes a significant barrier to mandating more frequent disclosures. They said a tailored approach would be more effective than a one-sizefits-all requirement for issuers to provide more frequent disclosure information.

Require Certain Conduit Borrowers to Comply with Corporate Disclosure Requirements

Four of 21 experts and 1 of 21 market participant groups we surveyed and several issuers we interviewed said SEC should require corporate borrowers that issue debt in the municipal market to comply with disclosure requirements for corporate issuers because this sector has been responsible for most payment defaults.[60] Although a few sectors of the municipal market with corporate borrower participation provide disclosure beyond that required by Rule 15c2-12, not all do. According to SEC staff with whom we spoke, requiring corporate disclosure of conduit borrowers would require certain statutory action to repeal Securities Act exemptions for certain types of securities; however, the Tower Amendment could remain in place. While the Tower Amendment restricts SEC from requiring prefiling information from municipal securities issuers, the restriction does not apply to conduit borrowers, as they are not municipal securities issuers. Whether a corporate conduit borrower is subject to registration and reporting requirements for public companies would depend on whether the corporate conduit borrower qualified for a specific exemption under the Securities Act.

Two market participant groups and an expert with whom we spoke suggested that applying corporate disclosure requirements to conduit borrowers would provide a risk-based approach to improving disclosure. They said focusing changes of disclosure rules on the highest-risk sectors of the market would improve investor protection in the areas of greatest need. One expert we surveyed said conduit borrowers should be required to provide investors with more information because conduit borrowers benefit financially from reduced interest rates on tax-exempt municipal bonds. The expert said eliminating exemptions for corporate borrowers could provide clarity to investors on what entities issue debt in the municipal market, and could provide investors with access to the same registration and disclosure information that otherwise would be available on the same entities if issuing securities in the corporate market. While eliminating exemptions for conduit borrowers could improve transparency, one small issuer told us there could be some costs to government issuers, as some local governments may be required to assume development costs. Conduit issuers agreed that eliminating exemptions could increase costs to conduit borrowers and cause some to leave the market—in theory, leading to lost economic development opportunities.

SEC staff have recommended that the exemption provided by Section 3(a)(2) of the Securities Act be eliminated for corporate conduit borrowers.[61] In 1994, SEC supported this option, but the current commission has not taken a position on this issue. SEC staff have been examining this issue as part of their ongoing study of the municipal securities market. MSRB staff said market participants reported that municipal securities with conduit borrowers in some sectors have been less compliant with continuing disclosure agreements than other types of municipal securities. They said planned improvements to EMMA could help users identify and track conduit issuances, which could aid conduit borrowers in managing their continuing disclosure obligations or help regulators and investors track securities with conduit borrowers.

Other Options for Improving Continuing Disclosure Could Be Achieved within Existing Regulatory Framework

Experts and market participant groups we surveyed and others with whom we spoke suggested other options for improving disclosure that could be implemented within the existing regulatory framework. These included further improving the functionality of EMMA and strengthening efforts to promote EMMA to issuers and investors. Other options included expanding SEC enforcement activities and improving the readability and usefulness of disclosure information by providing guidance or requiring use of plain English in disclosures.

Improve and Promote EMMA

Six market participant groups with whom we spoke and 4 of 21 experts and 3 of 21 market participant groups we surveyed told us EMMA was a significant improvement from the former system for distributing disclosure, and 2 market participant groups said its usefulness had improved since it was first implemented.

Members of a group representing issuers said the system provided issuers greater certainty about their compliance with continuing disclosure agreements, as EMMA allows issuers to verify what information they submitted to the system and where it was posted online. When using the former system, issuers mailed in paper documents and lacked the ability to see whether information was filed or if it had been categorized correctly. They said EMMA had made it easier to more accurately file disclosure information, as it was easier to associate disclosure information with appropriate identifiers (CUSIP numbers).

Nevertheless, 6 market participant groups we interviewed and 3 of 21 market participant groups and 2 of 21 experts we surveyed suggested further improvements to EMMA could benefit disclosure.[62] Suggestions for improving EMMA included making it easier for investors to find specific securities, making it easier for investors to determine whether financial information had been submitted, and ensuring that information was properly coded to appropriate categories and securities.

According to one market participant group with whom we spoke, further improving EMMA's functionality would reduce the time and level of effort required of EMMA users to understand the significance of the information provided. Two market participant groups representing issuers told us that while EMMA has made it easier for them to manage their investor disclosures and determine whether disclosures are publicly available, additional improvements would further increase the functionality and usefulness of the system.

MSRB staff agreed that further improving EMMA would encourage greater issuer discipline in complying with continuing disclosure agreements, because functionality improvements to EMMA could provide investors better access to disclosure information and, in turn, increase investor demand for disclosure in EMMA.

Four of 21 market participant groups we surveyed and 3 others with whom we spoke said regulators could strengthen efforts to educate issuers on their disclosure responsibilities. For instance, three market participant groups we interviewed told us some issuers have not yet submitted information to EMMA because they might not be aware of their disclosure obligations under their continuing disclosure agreements. Regulators discussed with us their efforts to educate issuers about EMMA. MSRB's primary education focus for the first year after launching EMMA was to inform and train issuers on their new obligations to file disclosure information to EMMA. According to MSRB staff, these efforts included providing industry conference presentations, developing webinars, creating a call center to provide support to issuers submitting information to EMMA, and posting a list of frequently asked questions on the MSRB website.

While these efforts have continued, MSRB has updated its issuer education focus from introducing EMMA to how to leverage EMMA to communicate directly with investors. In November 2011, MSRB launched a toolkit for state and local government issuers on its website, which included information on making continuing disclosure submissions to EMMA and how issuers can better use the information available on EMMA. While MSRB staff view MSRB's initial issuer education efforts as successful because frequent issuers are aware of EMMA and MSRB received positive feedback from the issuer community, they said additional work was needed to educate infrequent, small issuers. Four of 21 market participant groups and 1 of 21 experts we surveyed also suggested that regulators could strengthen efforts to improve investor awareness of EMMA, as the extent to which individual investors use EMMA is difficult to ascertain. More specifically, 7 of the 12 individual investors with whom we spoke did not use EMMA to obtain disclosure information because a few said they were not aware of EMMA and several said they relied on advisors for investment advice and information instead of conducting their own research.

Regulators said they expected investor awareness of EMMA to improve over time, and described the extent of their efforts to make investors aware of EMMA. In 2009, MSRB initiated an education and outreach effort to raise awareness of EMMA among investors and others who act on their behalf, and to promote use of the site by market participants. MSRB has used websites, social media, search engines, print and broadcast media, and public speaking engagements, among other things, to communicate to investors, issuers, and the broker-dealer community about EMMA. MSRB also requires that trade confirmations or other documentation associated with primary market transactions provide notice that primary offering disclosure information (official statements) is available through EMMA. Further, MSRB developed an online education center and in May 2012 launched an investor toolkit on its website. MSRB staff told us they plan to develop focus groups of investors to explore ways to improve EMMA, which could include how to improve investor education efforts. Additionally, SEC, FINRA, and others have promoted EMMA on various websites relevant to investors interested in purchasing municipal securities.

Expand SEC Enforcement Activities

Three of 21 market participant groups and 1 of 21 experts we surveyed, and 3 market participant groups with whom we spoke suggested SEC could expand its enforcement activities using its existing antifraud authorities as leverage to improve issuers' adherence with continuing disclosure agreements. As discussed previously, SEC does not have the authority to directly require issuers to submit continuing disclosure information to EMMA. SEC enforcement actions using its antifraud authority could encourage issuers to comply with their continuing disclosure obligations. For example, one issuer we interviewed said he was careful to comply with the continuing disclosure agreement, as he did not want to risk the city becoming the subject of an SEC enforcement action.

An expert and a market participant group we surveyed, and two market participant groups we interviewed discussed the potential benefits of increased enforcement activity. They said a few high-profile enforcement actions could improve disclosure compliance. For example, representatives of a national group that advises issuers on their disclosures said enforcement actions and interpretive releases were their main sources of guidance for preparing or advising issuers about disclosure information.

To be held liable under the antifraud provisions, issuers must make a material misstatement or omission in their disclosures or public statements (such as to EMMA or in a speech).[63] SEC has initiated enforcement actions against state and local governments for materially false and misleading disclosures they provided to investors in connection with publicly offered municipal securities. For example, SEC found that the State of New Jersey and the City of San Diego violated antifraud provisions by misstating or omitting material information about the annual funding of their pension obligations, which SEC alleged to be material information on which investors would rely.[64] To strengthen enforcement efforts in the municipal securities market, SEC created a municipal securities and public pensions unit in its Division of Enforcement in January 2010. Initial efforts by the division include identifying market activities that pose the greatest risk to investors and identifying potential violations.

Provide Guidance to Help Standardize Disclosure

Six of 21 experts and 8 of 21 market participant groups we surveyed suggested efforts by regulators to standardize disclosure information could benefit investors by improving the content and readability of disclosure. Their suggestions included that SEC establish disclosure guidance on ways to standardize the organization of information or highlight what information could be important according to the type of security or credit sector. Additionally, an investor suggested regulators develop a one-page template issuers could use to provide information most pertinent to investors, in an easily understood format.

Three of 21 market participant groups we surveyed and a market participant group and an investor with whom we spoke said additional guidance or templates could improve the readability and comparability of information disclosed in EMMA, improving investors' understanding of the information.

Additionally, an expert said such guidance, outlining broad categories of basic information all issuers should provide, would be particularly helpful to small or infrequent issuers that lack the resources needed to maintain an awareness of industry changes in disclosure standards. However, many large, small, and conduit issuers with whom we spoke identified potential challenges to providing standardized information. They said standardized formats could require different information from what is collected and maintained now, requiring changes that could impose additional costs on issuers through increased staff time, hiring additional expertise, and associated opportunity costs. Also, 1 of 21 market participant groups we surveyed was concerned that direct regulation of disclosure content and format by SEC or MSRB could have an adverse effect on the quality of disclosure information. That is, standardized information might provide investors with information that was too general to be useful.

SEC staff said they have been exploring different ideas to assist municipal issuers in improving disclosure as part of the staff's ongoing review of the municipal securities market. For example, SEC staff told us SEC could consider having a role in helping issuers determine what types of information would be useful for investors' decision making. While MSRB had not specifically discussed developing templates for disclosure in its long-range plan for EMMA, staff told us MSRB could consider possible options to help standardize disclosure using its authority over how information gets submitted to EMMA.

MSRB staff told us examples could include creating a template for baseline disclosure such as an online form for submitting information to EMMA, or providing guidance or best practices to show patterns of good disclosure and highlight good disclosure practices. Staff also suggested MSRB could consider developing an online library of links to websites with guidance and best practices developed by industry groups and regulators.

Require Use of Plain English

Three of 21 market participant groups and 1 of 21 experts we surveyed suggested federal regulators should require issuers to use plain English when preparing information for submission to EMMA. For example, they suggested issuers use plain language to describe financial information or the implications of event notices.

To some extent, issuers already have been following these practices. Municipal issuers that satisfy their annual reporting obligation (agreed on in their continuing disclosure agreement) by submitting an annual financial report prepared in accordance with GASB rules provide a management discussion and analysis.[65] Additionally, four of seven large issuers and three of seven conduit issuers with whom we spoke had made efforts to incorporate plain language into their annual financial reports and other financial information they posted to their websites. For example, three of seven large issuers said using plain language was a long-time goal. However, large, small, and conduit issuers with whom we spoke said cost factors, including potential liability under SEC antifraud authority, lack of internal expertise, and complex accounting standards, have made it challenging to summarize or interpret the disclosure information they provide in plain language. Because of these factors, one large issuer told us investors should seek assistance from brokers or financial advisors on interpreting financial disclosure information, rather than relying on issuers to provide plain language or summary information.

MSRB staff told us it would be difficult to enforce a requirement that information provided to EMMA use plain English, given the number and diversity of municipal issuers. They said it would be easier to mandate use of plain English if SEC had direct authority over municipal issuers.

MSRB and SEC Have Been Taking Steps to Address Some Options

MSRB has taken recent actions to improve the timeliness of disclosure of financial information, the frequency of disclosure, and the completeness of disclosure filings through improvements to EMMA with a focus on the system's functionality. Examples of recent improvements include the following:

- Filing date information—MSRB expanded the information underwriters report at the time of an offering to include the date by which issuers agree to provide annual financial information. This information is displayed in EMMA, making lapses in annual disclosure more transparent to users.[66]

- Voluntary information—MSRB also developed features in EMMA that allow issuers to submit different types of information on a voluntary basis, including monthly budget updates. Additional changes, which became effective May 2011, permit issuers, obligated persons, and parties providing disclosure on their behalf, to provide to EMMA additional categories of information including specifying a timeframe of 120 or 150 days for submitting annual financial information, indicating use of GAAP as established by GASB or Financial Accounting Standards Board (FASB), or providing a web address (URL) where additional financial information is available.[67] An issuer's agreement to participate in any of these voluntary undertakings would be prominently displayed in EMMA.
- Rating information—MSRB implemented a direct feed to EMMA of ratings information from two of the rating agencies that currently provide ratings on municipal securities. [68] According to MSRB, the rating agencies voluntarily provide ratings information to EMMA, which is updated automatically. Consequently, EMMA users who previously might not have been aware of rating changes affecting their securities could obtain timely and accurate information.

In addition to these recent efforts, in January 2012, MSRB issued its long-range plan for further developing the EMMA system.[69] According to MSRB's long-range plan, planned improvements reflect suggestions MSRB received from market participants and others through such venues as industry roundtables, outreach events, targeted meetings, and feedback through the EMMA website.

MSRB's long-range plan includes improving search capabilities to make it easier for investors to find securities. Planned changes would allow users to find specific securities information using information other than CUSIP numbers, such as keywords, map-based information, or hierarchy-based searches (for example, securities within a given state), and would allow users to conduct advanced searches within disclosure documents. The plan also includes ongoing work with the issuer community to develop additional tools and utilities to help issuers manage their debt portfolios and to promote more comprehensive and timely disclosure.

For example, MSRB plans to develop more flexibility for issuers to manage disclosure submissions and their appearance in EMMA. These new EMMA capabilities could enable issuers to compare the disclosure and performance of their securities with their peers' securities.

MSRB also plans to continue promoting awareness of EMMA and provide additional online education information for investors, including how to work with advisors, access pricing information, and use EMMA.

SEC's ongoing study of the state of the municipal securities market has focused on a range of issues such as primary and secondary market disclosure practices, financial reporting and accounting, investor protection and education, and market structure (including pretrade price transparency).[70]

SEC staff told us one purpose of the study is to identify risks in the market and what types of changes, if any, might be needed, including changes in the quality and timeliness of disclosure information provided to the market.

SEC staff expect to release their staff report in 2012, and include legislative, regulatory, and industry best practices and recommendations to SEC Commissioners for measures to improve primary and secondary market disclosure practices, measures to improve market practices, and associated regulation.

In addition, the Dodd-Frank Act required SEC to create an Office of Municipal Securities to administer SEC rules for municipal securities brokers and dealers, advisors, investors, and issuers, and to coordinate with MSRB on rulemaking and enforcement actions. SEC has been in the process of hiring an Office of Municipal Securities director and staff. SEC's fiscal year 2012 budget provides for five full-time staff; however, as of April 2012, the office had three employees.

AGENCY COMMENTS

We provided a draft of this report to SEC, MSRB, and FINRA for comment. SEC and MSRB provided technical comments, which we incorporated, as appropriate. FINRA did not provide comments on the draft report.

A. Nicole Clowers Director
Financial Markets and Community Investment

APPENDIX I: OBJECTIVES, SCOPE, AND METHODOLOGY

The objectives of this report were to (1) examine the extent to which information currently provided on municipal securities is useful and the extent to which existing regulation reflects principles for effective disclosure; and (2) identify options for improving the information issuers disclose to investors of municipal securities, and the related benefits and challenges of these options for investors and issuers.

To describe the extent to which information is useful for investors, we reviewed documents from the Securities and Exchange Commission (SEC) and the Municipal Securities Rulemaking Board (MSRB), including rulemakings, studies, statistical reports, staff reports, and a plan that described various issues concerning municipal securities disclosure. We reviewed the transcripts of SEC hearings on the state of the municipal securities market held in San Francisco, California; Washington, D.C.; and Birmingham, Alabama, on various dates in 2010 and 2011. We also reviewed 45 comment letters submitted to SEC as of January 25, 2012, regarding its study of the municipal securities market. We conducted a case study of disclosure information that we obtained from MSRB's Electronic Municipal Market Access (EMMA) system and made observations about EMMA's ease of use, the completeness of the disclosed information, and the ease with which certain information could be found in the disclosures. As EMMA became the central repository for primary market and continuing disclosures in July 2009, we reviewed 14 issuances that were offered between July and December 2009. The issuances reviewed included 2 issued by small governmental entities (a school district and a fire district), 2 issued by medium-sized governmental entities (a utility district and a city), and 2 issued by large governmental entities (a state and a city education board) for general-obligation debt issuances. One issuance was a general-obligation bond issued for a public hospital. The remaining 7 consisted of conduit issuances for a variety of projects, including an airport, solid waste facility, multifamily housing complex, stand-alone hospital, hospital system, continuing care retirement community, and nursing home. We also reviewed independent and academic studies on the usefulness of disclosure information and default studies from the three largest rating agencies as well as data on municipal securities defaults from an independent research firm to understand the risks to investors of municipal securities. We used data from Standard & Poor's and Moody's Investors Service to compare default rates for U.S. municipal issuers and global corporate issuers rated by each rating agency. We assessed the reliability of these data and found it to be reliable for this purpose. In addition, we worked through the American Association of Individual Investors to identify and interview 12 retail investors with diverse investment experience with municipal securities. We also interviewed institutional investors (including representatives for eight investment companies), professional analysts, a rating agency, an independent research firm, and groups representing market participants, including broker-dealers, bond lawyers, and municipal advisors. Finally, we interviewed staff of federal and state regulators, including SEC, MSRB, the Financial Industry Regulatory Authority (FINRA), and the North American Securities Administrators Association.

To describe the extent to which the information that issuers must provide reflects principles for effective disclosure, we reviewed federal laws and rules, agency regulations, and interpretive guidance that set forth disclosure requirements related to municipal securities. We reviewed SEC Rule 15c2-12, the primary SEC rule relating to underwriters of municipal securities. We reviewed information on SEC regulations for insider trading and that establish fair disclosure requirements for corporate securities to determine their applicability to municipal securities. We also reviewed SEC's antifraud authorities in the Securities Act of 1933 and the Securities Exchange Act of 1934, as well as provisions of these acts that exempt municipal securities from SEC registration and periodic reporting requirements. In addition, we reviewed MSRB's facility filing on EMMA, which establishes requirements for submitting disclosure information to the system. We compared these requirements with principles for effective disclosure and had two analysts review and come to independent judgments to determine the extent to which disclosure regulations reflected the principles. We used two sources for criteria. First, we used *Principles for Ongoing Disclosure and Material Development Reporting by Listed Entities* from the International Organization of Securities Commissions.[1] We believed these principles to be appropriate criteria for use in this context because our data collection indicated that continuing disclosure was a key issue for municipal securities disclosure. Although trading of municipal securities in the secondary market is infrequent, trading volume is substantial, indicating the importance of continuing disclosure. We did not use one of the principles—simultaneous and identical disclosure—in our analysis because the principle referred to making disclosures across borders, which is not important for municipal securities because the market is largely domestic and the securities do not trade on exchanges. Second, we used SEC's *A Plain English Handbook: How to Create Clear SEC Disclosure Documents*, which sets forth principles for preparing disclosure documents in easy-to-understand language.[2] We believed these principles to be appropriate criteria for municipal securities disclosure because our data collection indicated that readability was an issue for investors and a national organization representing state and local governments had suggested the principles to its members for producing municipal securities disclosure documents.

To identify options for improving the information issuers disclose to investors, we reviewed compliance and enforcement information from SEC and FINRA, including examination manuals for Rule 15c2-12 and MSRB Rule G-32, which set forth broker-dealer requirements for disclosures in connection with primary offerings. We reviewed data on examinations that found violations of the rule, and in certain cases, reviewed examination reports. Furthermore, we surveyed experts and groups representing issuers and other market participants, such as municipal advisors, broker-dealers, and professional analysts. The questions we asked experts focused on the regulation of municipal securities disclosure, whereas the questions we asked market participant groups focused on disclosure practices. This is because our initial interviews with market participant groups illuminated conflicts of interest that made it challenging to discuss options for regulating municipal securities disclosure. We recruited experts with career expertise in the municipal securities market and without obvious conflicts of interest, which we defined as the potential to benefit personally or professionally from the outcomes of our study or with a constituent they might feel the need to satisfy. Surveys for both groups asked for options to improve disclosure. We used a nonprobability sampling method to identify and select experts by obtaining referrals from other market participants, experts, and regulators. Although our results are not generalizable, our survey covered a diverse group of experts and market participant groups with broad and differing perspectives. We administered the survey to 26 experts and 29 market participant groups and received responses from 21 experts and 21 groups. We analyzed options according to what was mentioned most frequently and excluded suggestions that were not based on a correct understanding of the existing disclosure regime or were beyond the scope of our review. To control for small variations across the suggestions, three analysts reviewed and came to independent judgments to assign suggestions into various categories. To identify the types of benefits and challenges related to suggested options, we interviewed 20 issuers in three groups representing (1) large and frequent issuers, (2) small and infrequent issuers, and (3) conduit issuers. The group consisting of large and frequent issuers included representatives of three states, three large cities, and a county.

The group of small and infrequent issuers included representatives of five cities and a county with populations of 500,000 or fewer. The group of conduit issuers included representatives of three state housing finance agencies, three state health and educational facilities agencies, and a state bond bank. The issuers were geographically diverse, and represented entities from: California, Colorado, Florida, Georgia, Kansas, Maine, Maryland, Minnesota, New York, Oregon, Pennsylvania, Rhode Island, South Carolina, Tennessee, Texas, Washington, and Wisconsin. We also drew on information obtained from our survey and other interviews we conducted with investors, regulators, and market participants.

We conducted this performance audit from June 2011 to July 2012 in accordance with generally accepted government auditing standards. Those standards require that we plan and perform the audit to obtain sufficient, appropriate evidence to provide a reasonable basis for our findings and conclusions based on our audit objectives. We believe that the evidence obtained provides a reasonable basis for our findings and conclusions based on our audit objectives.

APPENDIX II: KEY FEDERAL DISCLOSURE REQUIREMENTS FOR PUBLICLY OFFERED MUNICIPAL AND CORPORATE SECURITIES

Table 2 compares key federal disclosure requirements for municipal and corporate securities. The information in the table is organized according to whether requirements apply to primary or second dary market disclosure, with requirements that apply to both presented first.

Table 2. Comparison of Key Federal Disclosure Requirements for Publicly Offered Municipal and Corporate Securities, as of June 2012

Key federal disclosurerequirement	Municipal	Corporate
Applicability of antifraud provisions[a]	Yes SEC is authorized to take enforcement actions against any person or entity that violates antifraud provisions.	Yes SEC is authorized to take enforcement actions against any person or entity that violates antifraud provisions.

Table 2. (Continued)

Key federal disclosurerequirement	Municipal	Corporate
Use of generally acceptedaccounting principles	No Issuers are not required to prepare financial statements according to generally accepted accounting principles (GAAP). There are no requirements covering the preparation of financial statements. Nevertheless, we previously reported that all states use GAAP for annual financial statements.[b] Utilization varies among local governments, where cash-basis accounting also is used. Governmental Accounting Standards Board (GASB) establishes GAAP for state and local governments.[c,d] Corporate and nonprofit obligated persons may use GAAP set by the Financial Accounting Standards Board (FASB).	Yes SEC requires U.S. public companies to prepare financial statements according to GAAP. SEC designated FASB as the GAAP standard setter for corporate filers. Auditors must conduct audits in accordance with the standards of the Public Company Accounting Oversight Board.
Regulatory review	No SEC is not authorized to require municipal issuers to file presale information with SEC prior to the sale of municipal securities.	Yes SEC staff may review a company's filings for various purposes. SEC reviews some registration statements and declares them "effective" if the company satisfies disclosure rules, at which time the company may begin to sell its securities. Sometimes, SEC staff do not review registration statements and declare them effective. Some registration statements are effective automatically. SEC staff selectively review filings, including periodic reports, and provide the company with comments in instances where they believe a company can improve its disclosure or enhance its compliance with applicable disclosure requirements. SEC staff view the comment process as a dialogue with a company about its disclosure. The Sarbanes-Oxley Act of 2002 requires SEC to undertake some type of

Key federal disclosurerequirement	Municipal	Corporate
		review of a public reporting company's ongoing disclosure once every 3 years for compliance, and SEC may take enforcement actions.
Disclosure repository	Yes MSRB maintains EMMA (Electronic Municipal Markets Access), an online repository for disclosures.	Yes SEC maintains EDGAR (Electronic Data Gathering Analysis and Retrieval), an online repository for disclosures.
Exemptions	Yes The following types of municipal securities offerings are exempt, in whole or in part, from Rule 15c2-12 if one or more of the following conditions are met: • principal amount is less than $1 million;[e] • maturity is 18 months or less; or • the securities are sold in denominations of $100,000 or more and meet standards for limited distribution. There is a limited exemption from Rule 15c2-12 for offerings of municipal securities of issuers with less than $10 million in outstanding municipal securities.	Yes Federal securities laws provide various exemptions from registration for the following securities or transactions: • offered and sold to residents of one state; • private offerings; or • sold through employee benefit plans. A public reporting company may terminate its periodic reporting obligations based on number of shareholders and asset value, or such obligation may be statutorily suspended.
SEC registration	No The Securities Act of 1933 exempts municipal securities from registration requirements.	Yes Offers and sales of securities must be registered under the Securities Act of 1933 unless an exemption is available.
Primary offeringdisclosure	Yes For offerings subject to Rule 15c2-12, the rule requires underwriters to obtain and review an official statement consisting of information about the terms of the proposed offering, financial and operating data that is material to an evaluation of the offering, a description of the continuing disclosure undertaking to which the issuer agreed, and information on any failure to comply with any continuing disclosure undertaking in the previous 5 years. Obligation to provide primary offering disclosure to investors is on the underwriter.	Yes For registered offerings of securities, SEC's requirements include a registration statement and prospectus consisting of information about the issuer, including financial information, the terms of the proposed offering, the most significant risk factors affecting the issuer, and the interests of experts or counsel that advised the issuer, among other things. There are securities

Table 2. (Continued)

Key federal disclosurerequirement	Municipal	Corporate
		offerings that are exempt from registration and therefore exempt from such disclosure requirements. The issuer is obligated to provide primary offering disclosure.
Continuing or secondarymarket disclosure content requirement	Limited Rule 15c2-12 requires, as a condition to underwriting, an underwriter to reasonably determine that an issuer or obligated person has agreed in writing at offering to provide ongoing notices of certain events and annual financial information and operating data. Agreements are enforceable only by bondholders and other parties to or beneficiaries of the agreement, if any. SEC cannot enforce the terms of the agreement.[f] The underwriter's ability to engage in subsequent offerings is affected by whether the issuer has complied with their continuing disclosure agreements for prior undertakings. The underwriter must reasonably determine that the issuer has agreed to provide certain ongoing disclosure and disclose in the official statement compliance failures with previous undertakings for the previous 5 years.[g]	Yes SEC requires public reporting companies to submit annual audited financial statements and unaudited quarterly financial statements. SEC also requires public reporting companies to file notices of certain current specified events.
Secondary marketdisclosure format requirement	Limited MSRB requires EMMA submissions in portable document format and to be accompanied by certain indexing information.	Yes SEC requires that information filed on EDGAR to be in plain text or HTML. SEC requires most filers to submit data in an interactive format, XBRL. SEC provides detailed written guidance on the form and content for various filing requirements.
Secondary marketdisclosure timingrequirement	Limited There is no federal requirement to provide annual financial information within a certain time frame after the end of the fiscal year. Rule 15c2-12, however, requires that the date be specified in the written undertaking of the issuer or other obligated person. SEC Rule 15c2-12 requires continuing disclosure agreements to include the provision of certain	Yes Annual financial information must be filed within 45, 60, or 90 days after the end of the fiscal year, depending on the type of issuer Quarterly financial information must be filed within 45 days after the end of the quarter. Current

Key federal disclosurerequirement	Municipal	Corporate
	event notices within 10 business days of the date of occurrence; however, the terms of continuing disclosure agreements are unenforceable by SEC.	event notices must be filed within 4 business days of the event date.

Source: GAO summary of SEC and MSRB policies, rules, and regulations.

[a]SEC has authority to enforce statutory provisions and rules that prevent fraud in connection with the offer, purchase, and sale of securities. SEC may hold issuers and others responsible for misstatements or omissions of material information from disclosure.

[b]See GAO, Dodd-Frank Wall Street Reform Act: Role of the Governmental Accounting Standards Board in the Municipal Securities Markets and Its Past Funding, GAO-11-267R (Washington, D.C.: Jan. 18, 2011).

[c] GASB was established in 1984 as an operating component of the Financial Accounting Foundation. GASB is recognized by the American Institute of Certified Public Accountants as the body that establishes GAAP for state and local governments.

[d] We previously reported on the role and relevance of GASB in the municipal securities markets. Stakeholders with whom we spoke found GAAP-basis financial statements to be highly useful for assessing the quality of municipal securities compared with other bases of accounting. Examples of utility that they cited included that GAAP-basis statements provided important information on topics such as pensions and postemployment benefit plans, and that the management discussion and analysis section and enhanced disclosures in the notes sections provided context on an issuer's financial position. However, views on the pension information (in particular, the appropriate way to measure and accrue cost for these obligations) have become widely divergent. In addition, GAAPbasis financial statements are complex and expensive to prepare and governments are not always timely in issuing audited financial statements. See GAO-11-267R. In 2009, GASB issued an invitation to comment on pension accounting issues, followed by a preliminary views document in 2010, and two exposure drafts of proposed revised pension accounting standards in 2011. GASB approved its revised pension accounting standards in June 2012. The new standards apply to financial reports of pension plans for reporting periods beginning after June 15, 2013, and to government accounting and disclosure of pension information for fiscal years beginning after June 15, 2014.

[e] SEC Rule 15c2-12 establishes requirements applicable to underwriters of municipal securities.

[f] An obligated person is any person, including an issuer of municipal securities, who is committed by contract or other arrangement to support payment of the obligations on the municipal securities to be sold in an offering. Municipal securities may be issued by a governmental issuer acting as a conduit for the benefit of a private-sector entity or a nonprofit organization. Much of the disclosure for these securities pertains to and is provided by the obligated person. Examples of such obligated persons include not-for-profit hospitals, multifamily housing developers, lessees of airport and port facilities, and companies and persons that are the recipients of the proceeds of municipal securities issued for industrial or economic development projects.

[g] Antifraud provisions of the Securities Act of 1933 and Securities Exchange Act of 1934 prohibit the omission or misrepresentation of material facts in connection with the offer, purchase, or sale of any security, including a municipal security. SEC has used the antifraud provisions to bring enforcement actions against issuers that misrepresented their pension liability in official statements (which also may be looked to as secondary market disclosure for previously issued securities).

APPENDIX III: PRINCIPLES OF EFFECTIVE DISCLOSURE COMPARED WITH CURRENT DISCLOSURE REGULATIONS FOR MUNICIPAL SECURITIES

We compared requirements for continuing disclosure in the Securities and Exchange Commission's (SEC) Rule 15c2-12 and SEC's antifraud authorities with principles for effective disclosure that were developed by an international organization of securities commissions, which included SEC, and certain plain English principles developed by SEC.[1] We found that the current municipal securities disclosure requirements broadly reflect the seven principles for effective disclosure.

Table 3. Principles of Effective Disclosure Compared with Current Disclosure Regulations for Municipal Securities

Principle	Is this principle reflected in regulation?
Allocation of accountability The issuer or obligated person is responsible for compliance with the continuing disclosure obligation.	Yes SEC Rule 15c2-12 requires, as a condition of an underwriting, that an underwriter must reasonably determine that an issuer or obligated person, if any, has agreed to undertake for the benefit of bondholders to provide annual and event information over the lifetime of the security. Federal regulators do not have the explicit and affirmative authority to require issuers to comply with this aspect of the agreement. However, security holders may enforce the terms of the agreement through bringing suit against the issuer or obligated person.
Continuing disclosure obligation Issuers or obligated persons should have a continuing disclosure obligation requiring disclosure of all information that would be material to an investors' investment decision.	Yes SEC Rule 15c2-12 requires, as a condition of an underwriting, that an underwriter must reasonably determine that an issuer or obligated person, if any, has agreed to undertake for the benefit of bondholders to provide annual and event information over the lifetime of the security.
Disclosure criteria Continuing disclosure of information should be fairly presented, not be misleading or deceptive, and contain no material omission of information.	Yes SEC's antifraud provisions apply to municipal securities and participants in the municipal securities market. SEC has used its antifraud authority to take enforcement actions against municipal issuers for disclosing misleading information about the size of pension obligations.

Principle	Is this principle reflected in regulation?
Dissemination of information Under the continuing disclosure obligation, issuers or obligated persons should ensure that full information is promptly made available to the market by using efficient, effective, and timely means of dissemination.	Yes SEC Rule 15c2-12 requires, as a condition to an underwriting, an underwriter must reasonably determine that an issuer or obligated person has undertaken to provide disclosure information on EMMA, which allows for prompt submission to the market.
Equal treatment of disclosure The information to be disclosed in compliance with the continuing disclosure obligation should not be disclosed to selected investors or other interested parties before it is released to the public. Narrow exceptions include advisors and rating agencies.	Yes Although no federal regulation specifically requires that all disclosure information for municipal securities be shared evenly with all investors, municipal securities, like other securities, are subject to SEC insider trading restrictions. Also, SEC Rule 15c2-12 requires, as a condition to an underwriting, an underwriter must reasonably determine that an issuer or obligated person has undertaken to provide disclosure information on EMMA, which helps ensure equal access to information.
Timeliness Issuers or obligated persons should disclose ongoing information on a timely basis, including: • prompt disclosure of material developments, and • annual information.	Partial SEC Rule 15c2-12 requires that as a condition of an underwriting, an underwriter must reasonably determine that an issuer or obligated person, if any, has agreed to provide notices of certain events within 10 business days and to specify the date on which the annual financial information for the preceding year will be provided. Although the rule requires that a date be specified in the undertaking for the filing of the annual financial information, it does not specify how long after the end of the fiscal year that date should be.
Use of plain English in official statements Official statements should: • use short sentences whenever possible, • use tables or bulleted lists (to present complex information) whenever possible, • use descriptive headings and subheadings, • avoid frequent use of defined terms (including acronyms and shortened names),and • avoid legal and highly technical business terminology.	No There are no regulations requiring the use of plain English in official statements, although some industry guidance recommends this practice.

Source: GAO summary of disclosure requirements for municipal securities.

Note: We compared the regulation of disclosure against principles for effective disclosure derived from two sources: International Organization of Securities Commissions, Principles for Ongoing Disclosure and Material Development Reporting by Listed Entities (October 2002) and SEC, A Plain English Handbook: How to Create Clear SEC Disclosure Documents (Washington, D.C.: August 1998). We determined that one International Organization of Securities Commissions principle, simultaneous and identical disclosure, was not relevant to the U.S. municipal securities market because these securities are not listed, but traded over-the-counter, and investors predominantly are in the United States. Thus, the concept of listing in multiple jurisdictions largely does not apply.

APPENDIX IV: PENSION LIABILITY REPORTING

Investors, a market participant group, and an expert told us that the reporting of pension liability in municipal securities disclosure documents could be improved with changes to accounting standards and financial reporting requirements. For example, several investors told us that Governmental Accounting Standards Board (GASB) standards, to the extent issuers adopted them, did not provide for reporting enough information, such as financial projections, that could help users determine whether an entity will have sufficient resources to cover future financial obligations. Consequently, there are concerns that future pension costs could crowd out an entity's ability to meet scheduled principal and interest payments on its municipal securities.

GASB and the National Association of Bond Lawyers have undertaken various efforts that could increase the amount of information reported on pension and other long-term liabilities, but the viability of certain proposals already has been questioned, and it is too early to determine how issuers will react to recent guidance produced by an industry coalition.

- In November 2011, GASB issued suggestions for broadening the information governmental entities report in annual financial reports to include projections of cash flow and long-term financial obligations (that is, bonds, pensions, other postemployment benefits, and longterm contracts) for a minimum of 5 years beyond the reporting period.[1] GASB issued these suggestions for public comment and anticipated that respondents could be sharply divided on the issue. Two of the seven board members did not agree with the suggestions. They said forward-looking financial information would be subjective, and they questioned the potential costs and benefits to governmental entities of preparing the information. They had concerns that the proposed suggestions could affect the timeliness of audited financial statements and some entities' willingness to report statements compliant with generally accepted accounting principles, or GAAP (for those entities that can choose whether to comply with GAAP).[2]
- In May 2012, the National Association of Bond Lawyers issued guidance to help issuers provide disclosures about their pension funding in primary offering documents, or official statements.[3] The guidance was approved by a group of 12 national organizations representing municipal securities issuers, underwriters, analysts, institutional investors, accountants, actuaries, and others. The

Government Finance Officers Association, which has produced disclosure guidance for its diverse membership of governmental issuers, has indicated it plans to approve best practices based on this guidance by October 2012. However, it is too early to determine what the best practices would encompass or the extent to which issuers would adopt them.

- In June 2012, GASB approved standards that amend accounting and financial reporting on pension plans. 4 Among other changes, these standards made more uniform the methodology used to calculate pension liabilities and costs, require governments to recognize their net pension liability on the balance sheet for the first time, and provide additional historical information about pension funding status. GASB believes the new standards will result in a more faithful representation of the full impact of pension obligations. We reviewed selected comment letters submitted to GASB regarding its proposals to revise its pension accounting standards, issued 1 year earlier in June 2011, and found that views on the pension information (in particular, the appropriate way to measure and accrue cost for these obligations) had become widely divergent.[5]

End Notes

[1] For the purpose of this report, municipal securities are debt instruments issued by state and local governments. Municipal securities also include certain types of nondebt instruments (known as municipal fund securities) that include interests in 529 college savings plans. Practices with respect to municipal fund securities are beyond the scope of this report.

[2] Board of Governors of the Federal Reserve System, Flow of Funds Accounts of the United States, June 7, 2012. Municipal securities are bought, sold, and underwritten by securities firms registered as brokers or dealers and by banks registered as municipal securities dealers (sometimes referred to as bank dealers). For purposes of this report, we collectively refer to securities firms and bank dealers that purchase, sell, and underwrite municipal securities as broker-dealers.

[3] In comparison, SEC reported in 2006 that there were 9,428 public companies in the United States with requirements to report information with SEC.

[4] Flow of Funds Accounts, June 7, 2012.

[5] Corporate and some nonprofit borrowers access the municipal market through governmental issuers that act as conduits to the market.

[6] SEC is the primary overseer and regulator of U.S. securities markets and administrator of federal securities laws. MSRB is a self-regulatory organization (SRO) created in 1975 with the mission to protect investors, state and local government issuers, other municipal entities, and the public interest by promoting a fair and efficient municipal securities market.

[7] In the Securities Acts Amendments of 1975, Congress prohibited SEC and MSRB from requiring any issuer of municipal securities, directly or indirectly, to file with them prior to the sale of such securities any application, report, or document in connection with the issuance, sale, or distribution of the securities. Congress further prohibited MSRB from requiring any issuer of municipal securities, directly or indirectly, to provide them or a purchaser or a prospective purchaser of such securities any application, report, document, or information with respect to the issuer. Pub. L. No. 94-29, § 15B(d), 89 Stat. 97 (1975) (codified at 15 U.S.C. § 78o-4(d)).

[8] Dodd-Frank Wall Street Reform and Consumer Protection Act, Pub. L. No. 111-203, §976, 124 Stat. 1376, 1924 (2010). The act also requires us to examine the municipal securities market, a requirement that we completed in a separate report. See GAO, Municipal Securities: Overview of Market Structure, Pricing, and Regulation, GAO-12-265 (Washington, D.C.: Jan. 17, 2012).

[9] FINRA is an SRO that regulates 98 percent of the broker-dealers that trade municipal securities. NASAA is a membership organization representing state securities agencies.

[10] For the text of SEC Rule 15c2-12, see 17 C.F.R. § 240.15c2-12.

[11] Section 15B(e)(4)(A) of the Exchange Act, as amended by the Dodd-Frank Act, defines the term municipal advisor to mean a person (who is not a municipal entity or an employee of a municipal entity) that (1) provides advice to or on behalf of a municipal entity or obligated person with respect to municipal financial products or the issuance of municipal securities, including advice with respect to the structure, timing, terms, and other similar matters concerning such financial products or issues, or (2) undertakes a solicitation of a municipal entity. According to SEC, the statutory definition of a municipal advisor is broad and includes persons who traditionally have not been considered to be municipal financial advisors. Pursuant to the Dodd-Frank Act, SEC has issued a proposed rule requiring the registration of municipal advisors with SEC, which includes an interpretation of the term municipal advisor.

[12] Disclosure required in the primary market, where these securities are issued, consists of official statements. Continuing disclosure is information provided in the secondary market, where these securities are bought and sold after issuance.

[13] FINRA does not have its own rulemaking authority over broker-dealers' municipal securities activities, but enforces MSRB rules for securities firms and bank regulators enforce MSRB rules for bank dealers. SEC enforces MSRB rules for all securities firms and bank dealers, and for municipal advisors, which may be integrated into or independent of broker-dealers.

[14] See S. Rep. No. 94-75 (1975).

[15] With limited exceptions, state and local governments issue bonds through a broker-dealer that underwrites, or sells, their bonds in a public offering to investors. In 2011, 157 broker-dealers underwrote municipal bonds and the 5 largest underwriters accounted for about 60 percent of par value issued, according to MSRB. MSRB calculated market share for long-term issues and excluded private placements and remarketing of variable-rate bonds.

[16] According to a 1993 SEC staff report, SEC adopted Rule 15c2-12 in response to disclosure deficiencies highlighted in the 1983 default of the Washington Public Power Supply System, which was the largest payment default in municipal bond history at the time. They also cited concerns that official statements were not being made available to investors at initial offerings. See SEC, Division of Market Regulation, Staff Report on the Municipal Securities Market (September 1993).

[17] An "official statement," which municipal securities underwriters are required to obtain and review, consists of information about the terms of the proposed offering, financial and

operating data material to an evaluation of the offering, a description of the secondary market disclosure undertaking to which the issuer agreed, and information on any failure to comply with any previous secondary market disclosure undertaking in the previous 5 years. 17 C.F.R. § 240.15c2-12(f)(3).

[18] EMMA may be accessed at http://emma.msrb.org.

[19] SEC Rule 15c2-12 enumerates events for which a notice is to be provided. The following events must be disclosed: (1) principal and interest payment delinquencies with respect to the securities being offered; (2) unscheduled draws on debt service reserves reflecting financial difficulties; (3) unscheduled draws on credit enhancements reflecting financial difficulties; (4) substitution of credit or liquidity providers, or their failure to perform; (5) defeasances; (6) rating changes; (7) tender offers; and (8) bankruptcy, insolvency, receivership or a similar event with respect to the issuer or another obligated person. The following events must be disclosed if they are material: (1) nonpayment-related defaults; (2) modifications to rights of security holders; (3) bond calls; (4) the release, substitution, or sale of property securing repayment of the securities; (5) adverse tax opinions, the issuance by the Internal Revenue Service of proposed or final determinations of taxability, Notices of Proposed Issue (IRS Form 5701-TEB) or other material notices or determinations with respect to the tax status of the security, or other material events affecting the tax status of the security; (6) the consummation of a merger, consolidation, or acquisition involving an obligated person or the sale of all or substantially all of the assets of the obligated person, other than in the ordinary course of business, the entry into a definitive agreement to undertake such an action or the termination of a definitive agreement relating to any such actions, other than pursuant to its terms; and (7) an appointment of a successor or additional trustee, or a change of name of a trustee.

[20] There are no detailed requirements regarding the content of an official statement. For purposes of SEC Rule 15c2-12, official statements should include a description of the terms of the security, financial or operating data, a description of the secondary market disclosure undertaking to which the issuer agreed, and other information. In addition, information included in the official statement is subject to the antifraud provisions of federal securities laws.

[21] Prior to July 1, 2009, investors could obtain disclosure information and documents from one of the four Nationally Recognized Municipal Securities Information Repositories, in most cases for a fee.

[22] See Governmental Accounting Standards Board, The Timeliness of Financial Reporting by State and Local Governments Compared with the Needs of Users (Norwalk, Conn.: March 2011). The study looked at the length of time it took to issue audited financial reports in compliance with GAAP for all states and a sampling of large and smaller counties, local governments, school districts, and special districts. Governments surveyed were not necessarily municipal securities issuers. Also, the study did not include annual financial information that was prepared using accounting standards other than GAAP.

[23] Users surveyed included municipal bond analysts, legislative fiscal staff, and researchers at taxpayer associations and citizen groups.

[24] See California Debt and Investment Advisory Commission, Municipal Market Disclosure: CAFR Filings: A Test of Compliance among California Issuers (CDIAC No. 11-04). This study tested whether issuers submitted certain annual financial information to EMMA according to the date agreed upon in the underlying continuing disclosure agreement. The study excluded information about the roles and responsibilities of obligated persons in submitting disclosure information. A commission representative told us that 59 of the 1,227

issuances studied were conduit issuances that, by definition, would have had an obligated person other than the issuer.

[25] In our case study of securities disclosures in EMMA, we did not systematically analyze the extent to which disclosures were readable because we could not establish objective criteria for identifying readability.

[26] For example, some investors said they need to make quick investment decisions when purchasing municipal securities in the secondary market because securities may be purchased by another investor within 2 hours.

[27] See Michael G. Bartolotta, "Municipal Securities Rulemaking Board's Recommendations for Update of 1994 Interpretive Guidance," MSRB comment letter to SEC, http://www.sec.gov/comments/4-610/4610-69.pdf (Aug. 8, 2011).

[28] A CUSIP number is an identification number assigned to each maturity of an issue intended to help facilitate the identification and clearance of securities.

[29] See International Organization of Securities Commissions, Principles for Ongoing Disclosure and Material Development Reporting by Listed Entities (October 2002). See also SEC, A Plain English Handbook: How to Create Clear SEC Disclosure Documents (Washington, D.C.: August 1998).

[30] See Michael G. Bartolotta, MSRB comment letter to SEC (Aug. 8, 2011).

[31] SEC Rule 15c2-12 requires that final official statements contain, if applicable, a description of any instances in the previous 5 years in which the issuer or other obligated person failed to comply, in all material respects, with any previous continuing disclosure agreement.

[32] The SEC release states that it would be very difficult for an underwriter to make a reasonable determination that an issuer or obligated person would provide information outlined in a continuing disclosure agreement if the underwriter found that the issuer or obligated person had on multiple occasions during the previous 5 years failed to provide continuing disclosure documents on a timely basis.

[33] The intent of the survey was to measure investor usage of SEC-mandated disclosure documents and satisfaction with plain English elements used in disclosure documents. The study concluded that because investors found disclosure documents to contain too much legal jargon and believed disclosures were too complicated and difficult to understand, investors often relied on a financial advisor or broker to read these documents for them. See Abt SRBI, Mandatory Disclosure Documents Telephone Survey, prepared for SEC Office of Investor Education and Advocacy (New York, N.Y.: July 30, 2008).

[34] According to MSRB staff, the information available through EMMA has an indirect, but significant, positive effect on individual investors who purchase municipal securities through broker-dealers. For municipal securities, broker-dealers are obligated under various MSRB rules to use information available through EMMA to (1) provide disclosure of material information to customers at or prior to the time of trade under MSRB Rule G17, (2) undertake a suitability determination in the case of a recommendation of a municipal securities transaction under MSRB Rule G-19, and (3) provide fair and reasonable pricing of municipal securities transactions with customers under MSRB Rules G-18 and G-30. SEC staff told us that EMMA is an important source of disclosure information for broker-dealers in relation to the advice they provide individual investors.

[35] A notice of failure to provide annual financial information is one of the types of filings that an issuer or other obligated person may make pursuant to Rule 15c2-12's requirement to provide annual financial information. See Municipal Securities Rulemaking Board, Municipal Securities Rulemaking Board 2011 Fact Book (Alexandria, Va.: 2012).

[36] MSRB staff said it can be challenging to identify securities subject to Rule 15c2-12 disclosure requirements for a variety of reasons, including the complexity of the exemptions. Prior to 2011, regulations did not require that the underwriter disclose whether the issuance was subject to the rule. Many official statements are submitted to EMMA for securities that are not subject to continuing disclosure requirements.

[37] Corporate debt securities that have been registered and whose issuers are subject to the periodic reporting requirements are subject to SEC disclosure requirements. Although default rates in the municipal securities market remain low, they can vary by sector. According to a 2011 report by a rating agency, over the last 30 years, two-thirds of all defaults have been associated with the industrial development, health care, and housing sectors. See Kroll Bond Ratings, An Analysis of Historical Municipal Bond Defaults: Lessons Learned -The Past as Prologue (Nov. 14, 2011). In response to these defaults, the market has demanded more frequent disclosure in some cases, according to MSRB staff as well as two market analysts. For instance, three of these sources told us that issuers or obligated persons in the health care sector frequently provide financial information on a quarterly basis. Based on our case study of disclosures, the issuer or obligated person for four of the five issuances from the health care sector provided quarterly or monthly financial information in EMMA.

[38] See Neil O'Hara and Securities Industry and Financial Markets Association, The Fundamentals of Municipal Bonds, 6th ed. (Hoboken, N.J.: John Wiley & Sons, 2012): 174-175; and United States Courts, "Bankruptcy Filings Highest Since 2006," May 14, 2010, accessed May 10, 2012, at http://www.uscourts.gov/News/NewsView/10-05- 14/Bank ruptcy_ Filings_Highest_Since_2006.aspx

[39] In the event of default, the bond indenture may provide for recoveries in one of two ways: (1) the borrower may cure the default and resume paying full debt service, or (2) collateral backing the bonds may be liquidated. Debt service payments also may be made by a third-party guarantor. The study includes defaulted securities from January 1980 through October 2002. See David Litvack and Mike McDermott, Municipal Default Risk Revisited, Fitch Ratings (New York, N.Y.: June 23, 2003).

[40] Notably, Jefferson County, Alabama, which filed for the largest municipal bankruptcy in U.S. history in November 2011, defaulted on a general obligation bond payment due in April 2012. Prior to the bankruptcy, the state court in Alabama had appointed a receiver for Jefferson County's troubled sewer system, receivership being a potential remedy that some states allow.

[41] Whether a particular security has these protections depends on the structure of the financing and the statutory authorization for the security. The authors conducted a 50- state survey of rights and remedies provided by states to investors in municipal bond debt. See James Spiotto, Ann Acker, and Laura Appleby, Municipalities in Distress? How States and Investors Deal with Local Government Financial Emergencies, 1st ed. (Chicago, Ill.: James E. Spiotto and Chapman and Cutler LLP, February 2012): 254-255.

[42] SEC staff told us that improved disclosure by municipal issuers could benefit individual investors and also may have positive effects on pricing and liquidity. In a previous report on the municipal securities market, we noted that municipal broker-dealers generally determine the prices at which they are willing to trade by making relative assessments of a security's market value. Broker-dealers with whom we spoke identified several factors as relevant to their pricing determinations, including the characteristics and credit quality of the security (which broker-dealers can infer by reviewing information from issuers' financial disclosures posted on EMMA). Broker-dealers stated that their ability to understand the credit risk of a

particular security rested primarily on their ability to obtain timely, comprehensive issuer disclosures. We also noted that while MSRB has increased the amount of information available to all investors through its EMMA website—including price information on past trades and issuer disclosures—institutional investors with whom we spoke generally had more resources and expertise to assess prices than individual investors. In particular, they had (1) access to more sources of pretrade price information in the form of offerings and bids provided through their large networks of broker-dealers, (2) access to more user-friendly posttrade information through third-party vendors and their networks of broker-dealers, and (3) more market expertise to help them incorporate other available information. See GAO-12-265.

[43] Bond insurance provides securities with the rating of the bond insurer and guarantees investors timely interest payments and, if the issuers default, the return of principal. According to Thomson Reuters data in the 2006 and 2011 Bond Buyer Yearbook, in 2005, nine highly rated bond insurers insured about 57.1 percent of new issue volume (51 percent of newly issued securities). By 2010, there was only one active bond insurer in the market, providing insurance to approximately 6.2 percent of new issue volume (12 percent of newly issued securities).

[44] Some analysts have expressed concern in light of the recent financial downturn about the financial stress placed on state and local governments by pension liabilities. We recently reported that most state and local government pension plans have assets sufficient to cover their benefit commitments for a decade or more. We also found that states and localities have implemented various changes to their pension systems since 2008 that were intended to help improve long-term plan sustainability. However, growing budget pressures will continue to challenge the ability of state and local governments to provide adequate contributions to help sustain their pension plans. See GAO, State and Local Government Pension Plans: Economic Downturn Spurs Efforts to Address Costs and Sustainability, GAO-12-322 (Washington, D.C.: Mar. 2, 2012).

[45] See Elisse B. Walter, "Regulation of the Municipal Securities Market: Investors Are Not Second-Class Citizens," speech at the A. A. Sommer, Jr. Corporate, Securities and Financial Law Lecture (New York, N.Y.: Oct. 28, 2009).

[46] See Arthur Levitt Jr., "Muni Bonds Need Better Oversight," Wall Street Journal (May 9, 2009).

[47] See Elisse B. Walter, "Statement at SEC Field Hearing on the State of the Municipal Securities Market," (San Francisco, California: Sept. 21, 2010).

[48] See Michael G. Bartolotta, MSRB comment letter to SEC (Aug. 8, 2011).

[49] SEC staff expect to release a staff report on the municipal securities market in 2012 that includes legislative, regulatory, and industry best practices and recommendations to SEC Commissioners for measures to improve primary and secondary market disclosure practices, measures to improve market practices, and associated regulation.

[50] GASB establishes GAAP for state and local governments. However, issuers of municipal securities are not required to prepare financial statements according to GAAP.

[51] See GAO, Dodd-Frank Wall Street Reform Act: Role of Governmental Accounting Standards Board in the Municipal Securities Markets and Its Past Funding, GAO-11-267R (Washington, D.C.: Jan. 18, 2011).

[52] Because of the number of issuers—estimated at more than 50,000—our examples only illustrate categories of costs that could affect issuers.

[53] SEC has statutory authority to establish financial accounting and reporting standards for publicly held companies, but has looked to private-sector standard-setting bodies to develop

these accounting principles and standards. For example, SEC had recognized the Accounting Principles Board as the authoritative source for GAAP until 1973. Since the formation of the Financial Accounting Standards Board (FASB) in 1973, SEC has designated FASB as the private-sector standard-setter whose accounting principles are recognized as "generally accepted" for purposes of federal laws for public companies. The Sarbanes-Oxley Act of 2002 established criteria that must be satisfied for the work product of an accounting standard-setting body to be recognized as "generally accepted." Sarbanes-Oxley Act of 2002, Pub. L. No. 107-204, § 108, 116 Stat. 745 (2002). In 2003, SEC reaffirmed FASB as the private-sector standard setter. Commission Statement of Policy: Reaffirming the Status of the FASB as a Designated Private-Sector Standard Setter, Securities Act Release No. 8221, Exchange Act Release No. 47,743 (Apr. 25, 2003).

[54] See Elisse B. Walter, "Regulation of the Municipal Securities Market: Investors Are Not Second-Class Citizens" (New York, N.Y.: Oct. 28, 2009).

[55] See Elisse B. Walter, "Remarks before the Forty-third Annual Regulation Securities Seminar," (Los Angeles, Calif.: Oct. 29, 2010).

[56] Corporate issuers adhere to a 60-, 75-, or 90-day reporting standard based on their size and market capitalization.

[57] Component units, according to GASB Statement 14 as amended by Statement 61, are legally separate organizations for which a primary government is financially accountable or other organizations whose relationship with a primary government is such that their exclusion from annual financial statements would be misleading. Both states and smaller units of government have component units. For example, colleges can be component units of states and school districts can be component units of cities or counties. A recent report by a working group from the National Association of State Auditors, Comptrollers, and Treasurers said the majority of state issuers lack control or influence over the preparation or timing of component unit audits. Large issuers told us it would be challenging to compile information from component units in shorter time frames, as primary governments lack supervisory power to require component units to provide financial information within shorter time frames.

[58] By auditors of governmental entities, we mean both government auditors and private-sector auditors of governmental entities.

[59] See Mary L. Schapiro, "Remarks at Investment Company Institute 2010 General Membership Meeting," speech as delivered by Andrew J. Donohue (Washington, D.C.: May 7, 2010).

[60] Survey respondents and issuers with whom we spoke did not advocate changes to the exemption for nonprofit conduit borrowers.

[61] Statement of the Commission Regarding Disclosure Obligations of Municipal Securities Issuers and Others, Securities Act Release No. 7049, Exchange Act Release No. 33,741, 56 SEC Docket 479 (Mar. 9, 1994). Section 3(a)(2) exempts from registration under the Securities Act certain types of industrial development bonds, which corporate entities typically issue through governmental entities. For the relevant staff reports, see SEC, Staff Report on the Municipal Securities Market (Washington, D.C.: Sept. 1993), and Disclosure and Accounting Practices in the Municipal Securities Market (Washington, D.C.: Jul. 26, 2007).

[62] MSRB has issued a long-range plan for further developing the EMMA system, which we discuss later in this report.

[63] SEC staff told us that the antifraud provisions of the federal securities laws are broad, and may be utilized against persons (including issuers, local officials, underwriters, and financial advisors) in cases alleging fraudulent statements and omissions in offering documents,

annual financial information, other statements, or disclosures made by municipal issuers, and, in some cases, public comments made by officials who make a material misstatement or omission in their disclosures or public statements.

[64] See In re New Jersey, Securities Act Release No. 9135 (Aug. 18, 2010); In re City of San Diego, Securities Act Release No. 8751, Exchange Act Release No. 54,745 (Nov. 14, 2006).

[65] GASB Statement 34 established financial reporting standards for state and local governments and established that the basic financial statements and required supplementary information for government entities should include a management discussion and analysis. Among other things, the management discussion and analysis should provide an analysis of the government's overall financial position and results of operations to assist users in assessing whether the government's financial position had improved or deteriorated as a result of the year's activities.

[66] MSRB staff told us that MSRB is prohibited under the Tower Amendment from reviewing disclosure content. Although a recent rule change would enable EMMA users to determine whether an issuer has submitted annual financial information in accordance with its pledge, users determine whether the content of the disclosure is complete. See MSRB Notice 2011-08 (Feb. 7, 2011).

[67] Issuers can indicate voluntary plans to submit to EMMA annual financial information within 120 calendar days after the end of their fiscal year, or as a transitional alternative through 2013, within 150 calendar days after the end of the applicable fiscal year.

[68] MSRB staff told us that MSRB has committed to providing ratings information on EMMA from any nationally recognized statistical rating organization that rates municipal securities, agrees to participate, and makes appropriate arrangements to do so.

[69] See MSRB, Long-Range Plan for Market Transparency Products (Jan. 27, 2012), available at http://www.msrb.org/About-MSRB/Programs/Long-Range-Plan-for-MarketTransparency-Products.aspx.

[70] As part of its review, SEC facilitated three field hearings to gather perspectives on issues facing the municipal securities market, held in-person meetings with some market participant groups, and received public comments. SEC held field hearings in San Francisco, California; Washington, D.C.; and Birmingham, Alabama. We previously reported SEC had planned to hold more field hearings, but was unable to do so because of budget constraints. See GAO-12-265. Instead, staff held a number of "mini muni" meetings, with a variety of municipal securities market stakeholders at SEC's offices.

End Notes for Appendix I

[1] International Organization of Securities Commissions, Principles for Ongoing Disclosure and Material Development Reporting by Listed Entities (October 2002).

[2] SEC, A Plain English Handbook: How to Create Clear SEC Disclosure Documents (Washington, D.C.: August 1998).

End Notes for Appendix IV

[1] GASB, Preliminary Views of the Governmental Accounting Standards Board on Major Issues Related to Economic Condition Reporting: Financial Projections, No. 13-3 (Nov. 29, 2011)

[2] These board members suggested alternatives, including broadening standards for reporting historical information and information about how to obtain the subsequent year's budget. They said this information could provide an indication of the future of a governmental entity and that historical data help users to make conclusions about a government's ability to continue to provide its current level of service.

[3] National Association of Bond Lawyers, Considerations in Preparing Disclosure in Official Statements Regarding an Issuer's Pension Funding Obligations, (May 15, 2012). Available at http://www.nabl.org/ uploads /cms/documents/pension_funding_obligations_ document _5- 18-12_b.pdf, as of May 18, 2012.

[4] The revised standards, approved as Statements 67 and 68, replaced previous pension plan reporting standards (Statements 25, 27, and 50). Specifically, Statement 67 revised guidance for the financial reports of most pension plans, effective for periods beginning after June 15, 2013, and Statement 68 established new financial reporting requirements for most governments that provide their employees with pension benefits, effective for fiscal years beginning after June 15, 2014.

[5] See GASB, Accounting and Financial Reporting for Pensions: An Amendment of GASB Statement No. 27, No. 34-E (June 27, 2011) and Financial Reporting for Pension Plans: An Amendment of GASB Statement No. 25, No. 34-P (June 27, 2011).

INDEX

A

B

C

P

Q

R

S

T

U

V

W

Y